Spring 1998 Edition

COLLECTOR'S
VALUE GUIDE™

Collector Handbook and Price Guide

Ty®'s Beanie Babies®

Collector's Name

Contents

COLLECTOR'S VALUE GUIDE™ and THE COLLECTOR'S POCKET PLANNER™ are trademarks of Collectors' Publishing Co., Inc. The Collector's Value Guide™ is not affiliated with Ty Inc. or any of its affiliates, subsidiaries, distributors or representatives. Any opinions expressed are solely those of the authors, and do not necessarily reflect those of Ty Inc. Ty® and Beanie Babies® are registered trademarks of Ty Inc. Teenie Beanie Babies™ and Pillow Pals™ are trademarks of Ty Inc. Product names and product designs are the property of Ty Inc., Oakbrook, IL. Illustrations are the original creations and property of Collectors' Publishing Co., Inc.

Front cover (left to right): "Spunky™," "Princess™," "Stretch™," "Rainbow™," "Smoochy™," "Hissy™."
Back cover (top to bottom): "Princess™," "Quackers™ (without wings)," "Prance™."

Managing Editor:	Jeff Mahony	Art Director:	Joe T. Nguyen
	jeff@collectorspub.com		*joe@collectorspub.com*
Associate Editor:	Jan Cronan	Staff Artists:	Scott Sierakowski
Editorial Assistants:	Gia C. Manalio		David Ten Eyck
	Melissa Bennett		Lance Doyle
	Scarlet H. Riley	Contributing Artist:	Joni Walker
	Nicole W. Blasenak		
Contributing Editor:	Mike Micciulla		

Illustrations by Joe T. Nguyen, David Ten Eyck and Sal LoNero.

ISBN 1-888914-19-X

COLLECTOR'S VALUE GUIDE™ is a trademark of Collectors' Publishing Co., Inc.

Collectors' Publishing Co., Inc.
598 Pomeroy Avenue
Meriden, CT 06450
www.collectorspub.com

INTRODUCING THE COLLECTOR'S VALUE GUIDE™

*W*elcome to the Spring 1998 Edition of the *Beanie Babies®* Value Guide!

Ty®'s Beanie Babies have captured the hearts of adults and children, and have gained international attention in newspapers, on television newscasts and throughout the Internet. When these little beanbag toys were introduced in 1994, who would have predicted they would become the hottest collectible in years?

Whether you're a passionate collector or a casual Beanie fan, the Collector's Value Guide™ provides all the latest Beanie Babies information:

★ **New January releases & retirements**

★ **Full-color pictures**

★ **Up-to-date secondary market values**

★ **The 10 most valuable Beanies**

★ **Variations and name changes**

★ **Hang tag and tush tag differences**

★ **Complete list of Beanie poems**

★ **Games, mazes and word searches**

★ **Info and photos of all Ty's Pillow Pals**

★ **"Create Your Own Dream Beanie" contest in back of book**

The easy-to-use Collector's Value Guide is designed to make collecting Beanie Babies even more fun than ever!

B eanie Babies, those adorable little beanbag animals, have found a place in the hearts of the American people – right next to baseball and apple pie. Everybody's talking about them – on television newscasts and talk shows, at social gatherings, at work, you name it! In fact, Ty's Beanie Babies are such a part of our everyday lives that it's hard to believe that they've been around for less than five years. Everyone loves Beanie Babies and the excitement shows no signs of slowing down!

THE EARLY DAYS

Beanie Babies were created by Ty Warner, founder of Ty Inc, which has been producing plush animals since 1985. He wanted to make a stuffed animal that kids could hold in their hand and be able to buy with their allowances. A world traveler, Warner wanted to bring animals from the four corners of the globe into a child's home and heart. Little did he know that what he was unleashing would have such a resounding impact on so many people.

The first Beanie Babies made their way to store shelves in early 1994. There they sat, working their subtle magic on all who came in. It didn't take long. People began to notice the winning faces on the floppy beanbag animals and took them home. It took a few years of steadily-growing momentum, but Beanie Babies became a full-fledged national phenomenon by the beginning of 1997. The "Beanie hunt" was on!

THE BEANIE FACTS

Beanie Babies are made in China and Korea. Each beanie baby is cut from a plush pattern, sewn and then filled with small round pellets. The animals aren't filled completely, however – that's how they get their playful floppiness. Because they are individually sewn, Beanie Babies have subtle differences which add to their unique character and charm.

Beanie Babies come complete with heart-shaped "hang tags." Those simple red tags with the Ty logo have become one of the most recognizable product markings ever. An unwritten code has been recognized by many Beanie collectors: never remove the tags if you are interested in the future value of your Beanies! Each Beanie also has a "tush tag" sewn into a seam on the animal (see page 75 for more about Ty tags).

BRING ON THE BEANIES!

The Beanie Babies collection now consists of 138 designs and Ty has been so prolific that it's often hard to keep up-to-date. From 1994 through 1996, Ty followed a pattern of releasing new Beanies twice a year – once in January and again in June. Retirements are typically announced at the same time as the new releases.

During 1997, the Beanie collecting world was constantly abuzz with rumors and anticipation regarding new releases and retirements. By year's end, Ty had announced three "rounds" of Beanie introductions and retirements (January 1, May 11 and October 1). In addition to the regular introductions, Ty made the surprise announcement in mid-October of the teddy, "Princess." The proceeds from the sale of this special teddy will be donated to the Diana, Princess of Wales Memorial Fund.

What will happen in 1998? No one knows for sure, and that's part of the fun of Beanie Babies! The first wave of introductions in January (announced on Ty's website on New Year's Eve) brought forth 11 new Beanies and nine retirements.

WHY BEANIE BABIES? WHY NOW?

Whenever anything becomes a wild success story like Ty's Beanie Babies, a natural question arises: Why?

1. Fun. Kids love 'em. Moms and Dads love 'em! Truck drivers and telephone operators love 'em! You can push them, pull them, pose them and throw them. Beanies even appeal to both little girls *and* boys, an impressive feat in the often gender-segregated toy industry (with "Barbie" representing one side and "G.I. Joe" the other).

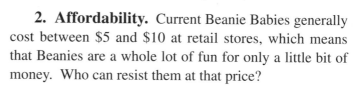

2. Affordability. Current Beanie Babies generally cost between $5 and $10 at retail stores, which means that Beanies are a whole lot of fun for only a little bit of money. Who can resist them at that price?

3. Scarcity. Depending on which side of the fence you're on, the Beanie Babies collection has either been "blessed" or "plagued" by the scarcity of many Beanies in stores. The truth of the matter is, however, that the incredible demand for Beanie Babies and the resulting shortages have created a "never-before-seen" excitement about Beanie Babies and their secondary market values.

4. The Internet. Much of the excitement about Beanie Babies has been fueled by the Internet, which wasn't available when the **www.ty.com** hula hoop or Rubik's Cube or even the trolls hit their stride. Now, however, fans all over the world can converse daily about their passion and hear up-to-the-minute news and gossip on the Web!

5. The Teenie Beanie Promotion. In an amazing synergy of events, Beanie collectors and McDonald's collectors descended upon stores from the country's number one fast food chain in April of 1997 to pick up Teenie Beanie Babies. The long drive-thru lines at many stores and the early shutdown of the promotion after only two weeks received extensive media coverage and brought the already hot Beanie Babies to a whole new level.

6. Variations. A new wrinkle in Beanie collecting was created as collectors discovered color and design variations for many Beanie Babies and decided that their collections wouldn't be complete without them!

7. Tags. The changes in Ty hang tags and tush tags have affected the secondary market value of Beanie Babies. Arguably more important to the development of the Beanie phenomenon was the addition of a birthdate and poem to each tag in 1996, which added a new level of fun to collecting Beanies.

Freckles™ style 4066
DATE OF BIRTH : 6 - 3 - 96
From the trees he hunts prey
In the night and in the day
He's the king of camouflage
Look real close he's no mirage!
Visit our web page!!!
http://www.ty.com

8. Cuteness Factor. Did we mention that Beanie Babies are just so darn cute?

BEANIE BABIES ARE HERE TO STAY

Beanie Babies are riding on the crest of the wave now, and it doesn't look like they're going away any time soon. The tremendous success of Beanie Babies has spawned countless numbers of imitators. But, as any true-blue Beanie lover will tell you, no one can make a Beanie like Ty.

Beanie News Flash!

In late 1997, Ty Inc. announced that two well-regarded former Enesco Corporation executives, Bob Ricciardi and Steve Ulrich, had joined the company. Enesco Corporation is the company that has introduced such fine collectibles as Precious Moments and Cherished Teddies to the market. Many of those "in the know" are optimistic that the expertise of these two men will help Beanie Babies remain a viable collectible for years to come.

Some people see Beanie Babies purely as a commodity, while others have a more sentimental feeling for them. But the delight that can be seen on children's faces as they play with their Beanies reflects the reason these little beanbag animals exist in the first place: they were made for the young and the young-at-heart. No one really knows how long the Beanie madness will last, but one thing is certain – the fun factor will still exist for Beanie Babies in the years ahead.

*M*ore Beanie Babies were introduced in January, with an additional 11 joining the 127 that were previously released. The new releases were announced on the Ty website (www.ty.com) on New Year's Eve. Each one of these adorable little critters would love to be your friend! Other big Beanie news for 1998 is the announcement of the official Beanie Babies club. Read on for details!

Britannia™ . . . "Britannia" is the latest patriotic teddy to join the collection, joining "Maple" (Canada) and "Libearty" (U.S.). This blonde teddy bear festooned with a red ribbon around its neck pays tribute to the glory of Great Britain. The Union Jack, better known as the flag of the United Kingdom, adorns her chest. You'd better plan your vacations now, because this teddy is a Ty Europe exclusive.

Bruno™ . . . "Bruno," one of two new dogs in the collection, is proud to be a terrier. The word terrier comes from the Latin word "terra," which means "earth." So it should come as no surprise that "Bruno" really digs playing in the dirt!

Hissy™ . . . A sensitive snake, "Hissy" knows there is a lot of bad press out there about no-legged creatures, and he's elected himself spokesperson for his species. A one-snake public relations firm, "Hissy" will go out on a limb to prove that he and his kind are friendly.

Iggy™ . . . "Iggy" has always loved adventure. Not one to let an opportunity pass him by, this tropical iguana hitched a ride in a pick-up truck heading north, and was last seen on Route 66, outside of Gallup, New Mexico.

Pounce™ . . . Judging by the name, this cat is not one to just sit around. One of two new cats, "Pounce" is similar in appearance to recently-retired "Nip," maybe they're from the same litter! This cat has brown fur with cream-colored spots on the paws, ears and face. Watch out or this feline will ambush you when you least expect it!

Prance™ . . . With a name like "Prance," this cat has happy feet! "Prance" is a gray cat with brown "tiger" stripes and patches of white on her paws, ears and forehead. The other half of the dynamic cat duo of new releases, "Prance" hops around and knows all the dance steps. Jitterbug, anyone?

Puffer™ . . . "Puffer" flew south from her home on the rocky coast of northern Canada because she couldn't stand the cold! A colorful little bird, "Puffer" looks like a cross between a penguin and a toucan! In fact, she's been known to pal around with "Waddles" on the weekends.

Rainbow™ . . . This chameleon is truly exotic-looking, with his big yellow eyes, fancy crest and shimmering coat. But don't let that air of royalty put you off, because once you get to know "Rainbow," you'll find he's really down to earth.

Smoochy™ . . . Looks like this frog has escaped from the rain forest. He's arrived just in time for Beanie fans, now that "Legs" the frog was retired in 1997. "Smoochy" loves people, so you'd better pucker up, because this amorous amphibian is gonna leap up and give you one right in the kisser.

Spunky™ . . . You don't even need to wind this cocker spaniel up, because he's ready to whir! This playful blonde puppy has long, furry ears and is just waiting for a playmate. With the addition of "Bruno" and "Spunky," there are now 15 dogs in the Beanie Babies collection.

Stretch™ . . . "Stretch" the ostrich had an image problem because her fellow mates were calling her "chicken." But this Australian bird overcame her fears, thanks to an assertiveness training course, and no longer hides her head in the sand.

AND IN CASE YOU MISSED IT

Princess™ . . . First arriving in stores in December of 1997, this highly-coveted violet teddy bear with a white rose stitched over her heart honors the late Princess Diana. All profits from the sale of "Princess" will go to the Diana, Princess of Wales Memorial Fund. Most retailers were limited to only a dozen of this special piece in the first shipment from Ty, but a limited supply is scheduled to arrive in stores in early 1998.

THE BEANIE BABIES CLUB DEBUTS!

Beanie Babies retailers and collectors are brimming with excitement over the January 1998 announcement of the "Beanie Babies Official Club." Collectors will be able to sign up for the club at retail stores designated by Ty as Official Beanie Babies Club Headquarters, so check your favorite store for sign-up details.

You will receive an official membership kit when you join. This will include a portfolio containing a membership card, a checklist, a newsletter, a membership certificate and Beanie Babies stickers. Members will also receive a free gift upon joining the club, a large, full-color Beanie Babies poster.

The Beanie Babies Official Club is sure to be a blockbuster hit among Beanie Babies collectors, especially in anticipation of exclusive Beanie Babies available only to club members. Run, don't walk, to your local store before you miss any of the club fun!

PILLOW PALS

The lovable Pillow Pals, another collection of plush animals from Ty Inc., are slowly gaining fans of their own. Pillow Pals are larger in scale than Beanie Babies and are stuffed with a soft, bouncy polyester material, just like a little pillow. These little critters are great for young children because they have embroidered features and are 100% washable. The Pillow Pals generally retail for under $15. Ty has introduced 25 Pillow Pals since 1995, including seven new designs for 1998.

New Pillow Pals: "Clover" the rabbit, "Foxy" the fox, "Glide" the porpoise, "Red" the bull, "Spotty" the dalmatian, "Swinger" the monkey and "Tide" the whale.

𝒥ntroducing the January 1998 Retirements!

On New Year's Eve, Ty announced nine new Beanie Baby retirements on its website (www.ty.com). Here's a complete list of all the officially retired Beanie Babies:

Retired on January 1, 1998:
    1997 Teddy, *bear*
    Bucky, *beaver*
    Cubbie, *bear*
    Goldie, *fish*
    Lizzy, *lizard*
    Magic, *dragon*
    Nip, *cat*
    Snowball, *snowman*
    Spooky, *ghost*

Retired on October 1, 1997:
    Ally, *alligator*
    Bessie, *cow*
    Flip, *cat*
    Hoot, *owl*
    Legs, *frog*
    Seamore, *seal*
    Speedy, *turtle*
    Spot, *dog*
    Tank, *armadillo*
    Teddy, *brown bear*
    Velvet, *panther*

Ty has officially retired 55 Beanie Babies since 1995. In addition to the nine 1998 retirements, Ty retired 17 Beanie Babies in 1996, as well as 29 Beanie Babies in 1997.

Retired on May 11, 1997:
    Bubbles, *tropical fish*
    Digger, *crab*
    Flash, *dolphin*
    Garcia, *bear*

Retired on May 11, 1997: (cont.):
  Grunt, *razorback*
  Manny, *manatee*
  Radar, *bat*
  Sparky, *dalmatian*
  Splash, *orca whale*

Retired on January 1, 1997:
  Chops, *lamb*
  Coral, *tropical fish*
  Kiwi, *toucan*
  Lefty, *donkey with flag*
  Libearty, *bear with flag*
  Righty, *elephant with flag*
  Sting, *manta ray*
  Tabasco, *bull*
  Tusk, *walrus*

Retired in 1996:
  Bronty, *brontosaurus*
  Bumble, *bee*
  Caw, *crow*
  Chilly, *polar bear*
  Flutter, *butterfly*
  Humphrey, *camel*
  Peking, *panda*
  Rex, *tyrannosaurus*
  Slither, *snake*
  Steg, *stegosaurus*
  Teddy, *cranberry bear*
  Teddy, *jade bear*
  Teddy, *magenta bear*
  Teddy, *teal bear*
  Teddy, *violet bear*
  Trap, *mouse*
  Web, *spider*

Ten Teenie Beanie Babies designs were available at McDonald's restaurants last year and all sold out by April 25, 1997:

Chocolate, moose
Chops, lamb
Goldie, goldfish
Lizz, lizard
Patti, platypus
Pinky, flamingo
Quacks, duck
Seamore, seal
Snort, bull
Speedy, turtle

*P*art of the fun of collecting Beanie Babies is in finding old and rare Beanies that collectors everywhere are searching for. Some Beanie Babies are selling for astonishing prices on the secondary market, with many pieces selling for hundreds, and even *thousands*, of dollars. Not bad for little plush animals that originally retailed for under $10 in stores.

This section lists the ten most valuable Beanie Babies, the roster which awakens longing in any Beanie lover's heart. Some Beanies in the top ten are color or design variations, while others are simply hard to find. Keep in mind that the secondary market fluctuates rapidly when it comes to Beanie Babies, and things can change faster than you can say, "1997 Teddy." In fact, one of the hottest Beanie Babies on the secondary market right now is "Princess," a tribute to the late Diana, Princess of Wales. "Princess" is a good bet to join the top ten once it is retired by Ty. Enjoy the hunt!

#1 Peanut (dark blue)
Market Value: $2,200

This rare royal blue pachyderm was shipped for only a month before the color was changed to a light blue. The light blue "Peanut" is still currently available.

#2 Quackers (without wings)
Market Value: $1,375

If you took the forlorn wingless "Quackers" home, you are one lucky duck! There may be as few as 1,000 of these in existence. The new version of "Quackers" has wings, however, and is still available in stores.

3 Spot (without spot on back)
Market Value: $1,300

Talk about misnomers. "Spot" was origi-nally produced without the expected spot, and is now highly sought after as a result.

4 Zip (all black)
Market Value: $1,250

That old superstition about black cats bringing bad luck obviously isn't true. This frisky black feline can surely be considered a good luck omen at prices like this!

5 Teddy (brown, old face)
Market Value: $1,200

This brown teddy with the "old face" also brings top dollar. The Beanie Babies teddies originally had eyes on the sides of their faces and a pointy snout. On the "new face," the eyes are placed closer together, and the snout is rounded out.

6 Nana
Market Value: $1,100

You'll go ape when you realize that that little mon-key sitting on your shelf is actually worth more than its weight in bananas! In 1995, "Nana" had his name changed to "Bongo," and he's still in the monkey business under that new alias!

#7 Brownie
Market Value: **$1,050**

One of the "Original 9" Beanie Babies, this brown bear's name changed to "Cubbie" in 1994.

#8 Slither
Market Value: **$975**

"Slither" has snaked his way into the top ten. His camouflage colors may allow him to blend into his surroundings, but nowadays, owners of "Slither" are seeing only green.

#9 Humphrey
Market Value: **$950**

Considered "undesirable" just a couple of years ago, "Humphrey" is one camel that a lot of folks are wishing they had right now.

#10 Peking
Market Value: **$925**

"Peking" the panda bear was only produced for a year before being retired. Now this exotic bear is as hard to find as its namesake.

*I*t's easy to determine the current value of your Beanie Babies collection:

Be sure to use a pencil when adding up the total value of your collection. Every time you buy a new Beanie, you'll want to record its value and watch your "Grand Total" grow!

| 1 | #4200 |

1997 Teddy™
Bear • Born: 12-25-96
Issued: 1997 • Retired: 1998
○ Got it! • Paid: $____
Market Value: **$75**

1. For each Beanie Babies plush animal you own, check off the "Got It!" box and write down the price you paid on the "Paid" line. For current Beanies, the "Market Value" will be the same as the price paid. Note: Only retired Beanies and variations are listed with secondary market values, although many current Beanies sell for "higher than retail" prices on the secondary market.

2. Find the secondary market value for each retired Beanie you own on its "Market Value" line ("N/E" = not established). If there are variations, determine which version you own.

3. Add the "Market Value" of each Beanie you own and write the sum in the "Value Totals" box on each page.

4. On page 64, write in your totals from the Beanie pages, then add the sums together to get the "Grand Total" of your Beanie collection!

1 #4200

1997 Teddy™
Bear • Born: 12-25-96
Issued: 1997 • Retired: 1998
○ Got it! • Paid: $____
Market Value: **$75**

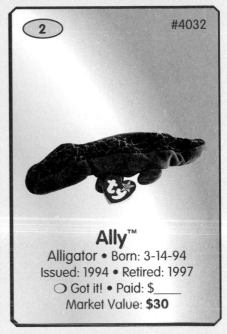

2 #4032

Ally™
Alligator • Born: 3-14-94
Issued: 1994 • Retired: 1997
○ Got it! • Paid: $____
Market Value: **$30**

3 #4074

Baldy™
Eagle • Born: 2-17-96
Issued: 1997 • Current
○ Got it! • Paid: $____
Market Value: $____

4 #4035

Batty™
Bat • Born: 10-29-96
Issued: 1997 • Current
○ Got it! • Paid: $____
Market Value: $____

COLLECTOR'S
VALUE GUIDE™

Value
Totals _____

5   #4109

Bernie™
St. Bernard • Born: 10-3-96
Issued: 1997 • Current
○ Got it! • Paid: $_____
Market Value: $_____

6   #4009

Bessie™
Cow • Born: 6-27-95
Issued: 1995 • Retired: 1997
○ Got it! • Paid: $_____
Market Value: **$50**

7   #4011

Blackie™
Bear • Born 7-15-94
Issued: 1994 • Current
○ Got it! • Paid: $_____
Market Value: $_____

8   #4163

Blizzard™
Tiger • Born: 12-12-96
Issued: 1997 • Current
○ Got it! • Paid: $_____
Market Value: $_____

Value
Totals _____

COLLECTOR'S
VALUE GUIDE™

9 #4001

Bones™
Dog • Born: 1-18-94
Issued: 1994 • Current
○ Got it! • Paid: $____
Market Value: $____

10 #4067

a

b

c

Bongo™
Monkey • Born: 8-17-95
Issued: 1995 • Current
○ Got it! • Paid: $____
Market Value:
a. Tan tail – $____
b. Brown tail – $85
c. "Nana" variation – $1,100

11 #4601

Britannia™
European Bear • Born: N/A
Issued: 1998 • Current
○ Got it! • Paid: $____
Market Value: $____

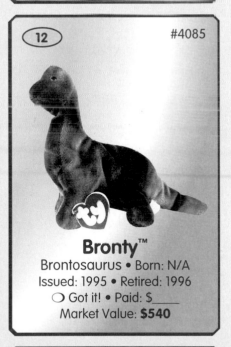

12 #4085

Bronty™
Brontosaurus • Born: N/A
Issued: 1995 • Retired: 1996
○ Got it! • Paid: $____
Market Value: **$540**

Value
Totals _____

13 #4010

Brownie™
(name changed to "Cubbie" in 1994)
Bear • Born: N/A
Issued: 1994*
Out of Production 1994
○ Got it! • Paid: $_____
Market Value: **$1,050**
* one of the "Original 9"

14 #4183

Bruno™
Terrier • Born: 9-9-97
Issued: 1998 • Current
○ Got it! • Paid: $_____
Market Value: **$_____**

15 #4078

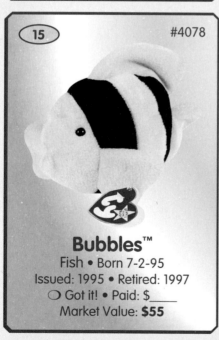

Bubbles™
Fish • Born 7-2-95
Issued: 1995 • Retired: 1997
○ Got it! • Paid: $_____
Market Value: **$55**

16 #4016

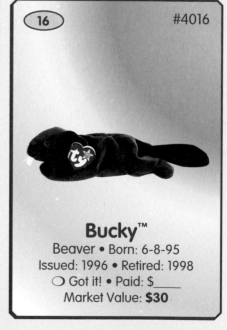

Bucky™
Beaver • Born: 6-8-95
Issued: 1996 • Retired: 1998
○ Got it! • Paid: $_____
Market Value: **$30**

Value
Totals _____

COLLECTOR'S
VALUE GUIDE™

17   #4045

Bumble™
Bee • Born: 10-16-95
Issued: 1995 • Retired 1996
○ Got it! • Paid: $____
Market Value: **$350**

18   #4071

Caw™
Crow • Born: N/A
Issued: 1995 • Retired: 1996
○ Got it! • Paid: $____
Market Value: **$395**

19   #4012

Chilly™
Polar Bear • Born: N/A
Issued: 1995 • Retired: 1996
○ Got it! • Paid: $____
Market Value: **$915**

20   #4121

Chip™
Cat • Born 1-26-96
Issued: 1997 • Current
○ Got it! • Paid: $____
Market Value: $____

COLLECTOR'S
VALUE GUIDE™

Value
Totals _____

21 #4015

Chocolate™
Moose • Born: 4-27-93
Issued: 1994* • Current
○ Got it! • Paid: $____
Market Value: $____
* one of the "Original 9"

22 #4019

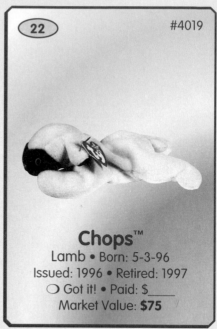

Chops™
Lamb • Born: 5-3-96
Issued: 1996 • Retired: 1997
○ Got it! • Paid: $____
Market Value: $75

23 #4083

Claude™
Crab • Born: 9-3-96
Issued: 1997 • Current
○ Got it! • Paid: $____
Market Value: $____

24 #4160

Congo™
Gorilla • Born 11-9-96
Issued: 1996 • Current
○ Got it! • Paid: $____
Market Value: $____

Value
Totals _____

COLLECTOR'S
VALUE GUIDE™

(25)   #4079

Coral™
Fish • Born 3-2-95
Issued: 1995 • Retired: 1997
○ Got it! • Paid: $_____
Market Value. **$80**

(26)   #4130

Crunch™
Shark • Born: 1-13-96
Issued: 1997 • Current
○ Got it! • Paid: $_____
Market Value: $_____

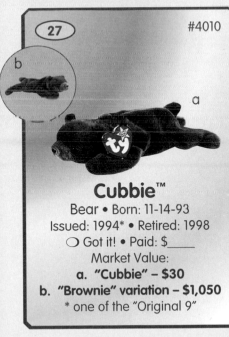

(27)   #4010

b

a

Cubbie™
Bear • Born: 11-14-93
Issued: 1994* • Retired: 1998
○ Got it! • Paid: $_____
Market Value:
a. "Cubbie" – $30
b. "Brownie" variation – $1,050
* one of the "Original 9"

(28)   #4052

Curly™
Bear • Born: 4-12-96
Issued: 1996 • Current
○ Got it! • Paid: $_____
Market Value: $_____

Value
Totals _____

29   #4006

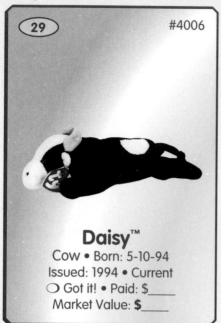

Daisy™
Cow • Born: 5-10-94
Issued: 1994 • Current
○ Got it! • Paid: $____
Market Value: $____

30   #4008

a

b

c

Derby™
Horse • Born: 9-16-95
Issued: 1995 • Current
○ Got it! • Paid: $____
Market Value:
a. White spot on forehead – $____
b. Coarse mane & tail – N/E
c. Fine mane & tail – $800

31   #4027

b

a

Digger™
Crab • Born: 8-23-95
Issued: 1995 • Retired: 1997
○ Got it! • Paid: $____
Market Value:
a. Red – $65
b. Orange – $380

32   #4110

Doby™
Doberman • Born: 10-9-96
Issued: 1997 • Current
○ Got it! • Paid: $____
Market Value: $____

Value
Totals _____

COLLECTOR'S
VALUE GUIDE™

33   #4171

Doodle™
(name changed to "Strut" in 1997)
Rooster • Born: 3-8-96
Issued: 1997
Out of Production 1997
○ Got it! • Paid: $____
Market Value: **$45**

34   #4100

Dotty™
Dalmatian • Born: 10-17-96
Issued: 1997 • Current
○ Got it! • Paid: $____
Market Value: $____

35   #4018

Ears™
Bunny • Born: 4-18-95
Issued: 1996 • Current
○ Got it! • Paid: $____
Market Value: $____

36   #4180

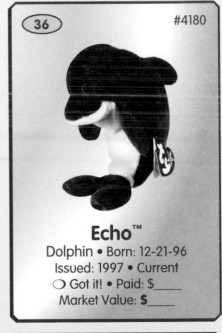

Echo™
Dolphin • Born: 12-21-96
Issued: 1997 • Current
○ Got it! • Paid: $____
Market Value: $____

COLLECTOR'S
VALUE GUIDE™

Value
Totals _____

My Beanie Babies® Collection

37   #4021

Flash™
Dolphin • Born: 5-13-93
Issued: 1994* • Retired: 1997
○ Got it! • Paid: $____
Market Value: **$65**
* one of the "Original 9"

38   #4125

Fleece™
Lamb • Born: 3-21-96
Issued: 1997 • Current
○ Got it! • Paid: $____
Market Value: **$____**

39   #4012

Flip™
Cat • Born: 2-28-95
Issued: 1996 • Retired: 1997
○ Got it! • Paid: $____
Market Value: **$40**

40   #4118

Floppity™
Bunny • Born: 5-28-96
Issued: 1997 • Current
○ Got it! • Paid: $____
Market Value: **$____**

Value
Totals _____

COLLECTOR'S
VALUE GUIDE™

41   #4043

Flutter™
Butterfly • Born: N/A
Issued: 1995 • Retired: 1996
○ Got it! • Paid: $_____
Market Value: **$475**

42   #4066

Freckles™
Leopard • Born: 6-3-96
Issued: 1996 • Current
○ Got it! • Paid: $_____
Market Value: $_____

43   #4051

Garcia™
Bear • Born: 8-1-95
Issued: 1996 • Retired: 1997
○ Got it! • Paid: $_____
Market Value: **$100**

44   #4034

Gobbles™
Turkey • Born: 11-27-96
Issued: 1997 • Current
○ Got it! • Paid: $_____
Market Value: $_____

COLLECTOR'S
VALUE GUIDE™

Value
Totals _____

45   #4023

Goldie™
Goldfish • Born: 11-14-94
Issued: 1994 • Retired: 1998
○ Got it! • Paid: $____
Market Value: **$25**

46   #4126

Gracie™
Swan • Born: 6-17-96
Issued: 1997 • Current
○ Got it! • Paid: $____
Market Value: $____

47   #4092

Grunt™
Razorback • Born: 7-19-95
Issued: 1996 • Retired: 1997
○ Got it! • Paid: $____
Market Value: **$90**

48   #4061

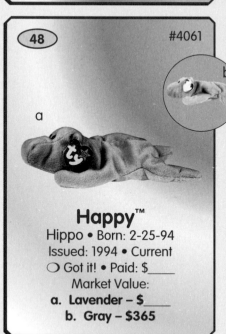

a

b

Happy™
Hippo • Born: 2-25-94
Issued: 1994 • Current
○ Got it! • Paid: $____
Market Value:
a. **Lavender – $____**
b. **Gray – $365**

Value
Totals _____

COLLECTOR'S
VALUE GUIDE™

49 #4119

Hippity™
Bunny • Born: 6-1-96
Issued: 1997 • Current
○ Got it! • Paid: $_____
Market Value: $_____

50 #4185

Hissy™
Snake • Born: 4-4-97
Issued: 1998 • Current
○ Got it! • Paid: $_____
Market Value: $_____

51 #4073

Hoot™
Owl • Born: 8-9-95
Issued: 1996 • Retired: 1997
○ Got it! • Paid: $_____
Market Value: **$40**

52 #4117

Hoppity™
Bunny • Born: 4-3-96
Issued: 1997 • Current
○ Got it! • Paid: $_____
Market Value: $_____

COLLECTOR'S
VALUE GUIDE™

Value
Totals _____

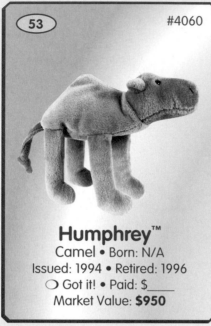

53 #4060

Humphrey™
Camel • Born: N/A
Issued: 1994 • Retired: 1996
◯ Got it! • Paid: $____
Market Value: **$950**

54 #4038

Iggy™
Iguana • Born: 8-12-97
Issued: 1998 • Current
◯ Got it! • Paid: $____
Market Value: **$____**

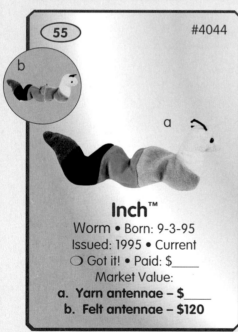

55 #4044

b

a

Inch™
Worm • Born: 9-3-95
Issued: 1995 • Current
◯ Got it! • Paid: $____
Market Value:
a. Yarn antennae – $____
b. Felt antennae – $120

56 #4028

a

b

Inky™
Octopus • Born: 11-29-94
Issued: 1994 • Current
◯ Got it! • Paid: $____
Market Value:
a. Pink – $____
b. Tan – $395

Value
Totals _____

COLLECTOR'S
VALUE GUIDE™

57 #4082

Jolly™
Walrus • Born: 12-2-96
Issued: 1997 • Current
○ Got it! • Paid: $____
Market Value. $____

58 #4070

Kiwi™
Toucan • Born: 9-16-95
Issued: 1995 • Retired: 1997
○ Got it! • Paid: $____
Market Value: **$80**

59 #4085

Lefty™
Donkey • Born: 7-4-96
Issued: 1996 • Retired: 1997
○ Got it! • Paid: $____
Market Value: **$110**

60 #4020

Legs™
Frog • Born: 4-25-93
Issued: 1994* • Retired: 1997
○ Got it! • Paid: $____
Market Value: **$45**
* one of the "Original 9"

COLLECTOR'S
VALUE GUIDE™

Value
Totals _____

My Beanie Babies® Collection

61   #4057

Libearty™
Bear • Born: Summer 1996
Issued: 1996 • Retired: 1997
○ Got it! • Paid: $____
Market Value: **$115**

62   #4033

Lizzy™
Lizard • Born: 5-11-95
Issued: 1995 • Retired: 1998
○ Got it! • Paid: $____
Market Value:
a. **Blue/yellow – $25**
b. **Tie-dye – $525**

63   #4040

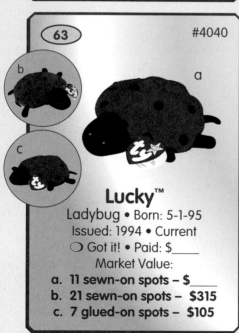

Lucky™
Ladybug • Born: 5-1-95
Issued: 1994 • Current
○ Got it! • Paid: $____
Market Value:
a. **11 sewn-on spots – $____**
b. **21 sewn-on spots – $315**
c. **7 glued-on spots – $105**

64   #4088

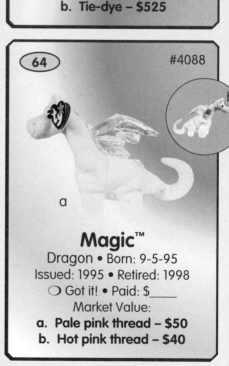

Magic™
Dragon • Born: 9-5-95
Issued: 1995 • Retired: 1998
○ Got it! • Paid: $____
Market Value:
a. **Pale pink thread – $50**
b. **Hot pink thread – $40**

Value
Totals _____

65   #4081

Manny™
Manatee • Born: 6-8-95
Issued: 1996 • Retired: 1997
○ Got it! • Paid: $____
Market Value: **$90**

66   #4600

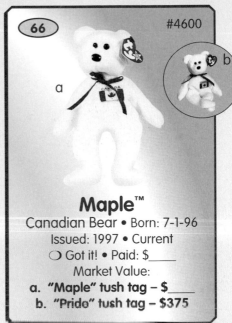

a

b

Maple™
Canadian Bear • Born: 7-1-96
Issued: 1997 • Current
○ Got it! • Paid: $____
Market Value:
a. "Maple" tush tag – $____
b. "Pride" tush tag – **$375**

67   #4162

Mel™
Koala • Born: 1-15-96
Issued: 1997 • Current
○ Got it! • Paid: $____
Market Value: $____

68   #4007

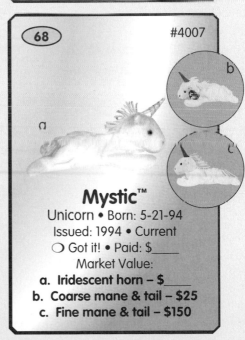

a

b

c

Mystic™
Unicorn • Born: 5-21-94
Issued: 1994 • Current
○ Got it! • Paid: $____
Market Value:
a. Iridescent horn – $____
b. Coarse mane & tail – $25
c. Fine mane & tail – $150

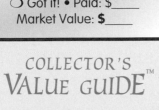

COLLECTOR'S
VALUE GUIDE™

Value
Totals _____

My Beanie Babies® Collection

69   #4067

Nana™
(name changed to "Bongo" in 1995)
Monkey • Born: N/A
Issued: 1995
Out of Production 1995
○ Got it! • Paid: $____
Market Value: **$1,100**

70   #4104

Nanook™
Husky • Born: 11-21-96
Issued: 1997 • Current
○ Got it! • Paid: $____
Market Value: $____

71   #4003

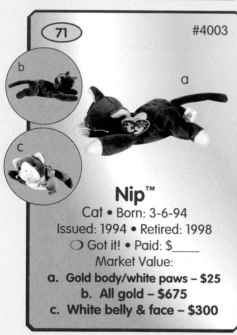

a

Nip™
Cat • Born: 3-6-94
Issued: 1994 • Retired: 1998
○ Got it! • Paid: $____
Market Value:
a. **Gold body/white paws – $25**
b. **All gold – $675**
c. **White belly & face – $300**

72   #4114

Nuts™
Squirrel • Born: 1-21-96
Issued: 1997 • Current
○ Got it! • Paid: $____
Market Value: $____

Value
Totals _____

COLLECTOR'S
VALUE GUIDE™

73   #4025

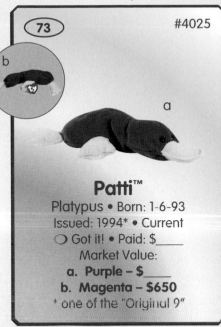

b

a

Patti™
Platypus • Born: 1-6-93
Issued: 1994* • Current
○ Got it! • Paid: $____
Market Value:
a. Purple – $____
b. Magenta – $650
* one of the "Original 9"

74   #4053

Peace™
Bear • Born: 2-1-96
Issued: 1997 • Current
○ Got it! • Paid: $____
Market Value: $____

75   #4062

b

a

Peanut™
Elephant • Born: 1-25-95
Issued: 1995 • Current
○ Got it! • Paid: $____
Market Value:
a. Light blue – $____
b. Dark blue – $2,200

76   #4013

Peking™
Panda • Born: N/A
Issued: 1994 • Retired: 1996
○ Got it! • Paid: $____
Market Value: **$925**

COLLECTOR'S
VALUE GUIDE™

Value
Totals _____

77 — #4026

Pinchers™
Lobster • Born: 6-19-93
Issued: 1994* • Current
○ Got it! • Paid: $____
Market Value: $____
* one of the "Original 9"

78 — #4072

Pinky™
Flamingo • Born: 2-13-95
Issued: 1995 • Current
○ Got it! • Paid: $____
Market Value: $____

79 — #4161

Pouch™
Kangaroo • Born: 11-6-96
Issued: 1997 • Current
○ Got it! • Paid: $____
Market Value: $____

80 — #4122

Pounce™
Cat • Born: 8-28-97
Issued: 1998 • Current
○ Got it! • Paid: $____
Market Value: $____

Value
Totals _____

COLLECTOR'S
VALUE GUIDE™

81   #4123

Prance™
Cat • Born: 11-20-97
Issued: 1998 • Current
○ Got it! • Paid: $____
Market Value: $____

82   #4300

Princess™
Bear • Born: N/A
Issued: 1997 • Current
○ Got it! • Paid: $____
Market Value: $____

83   #4181

Puffer™
Puffin • Born: 11-3-97
Issued: 1998 • Current
○ Got it! • Paid: $____
Market Value: $____

84   #4106

Pugsly™
Pug • Born: 5-2-96
Issued: 1997 • Current
○ Got it! • Paid: $____
Market Value: $____

COLLECTOR'S
VALUE GUIDE™

Value
Totals _____

My Beanie Babies® Collection

85   #4024

b   a

Quackers™
Duck • Born: 4-19-94
Issued: 1994 • Current
○ Got it! • Paid: $_____
Market Value:
a. With wings – $_____
b. Without wings – $1,375

86   #4091

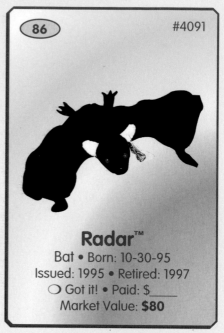

Radar™
Bat • Born: 10-30-95
Issued: 1995 • Retired: 1997
○ Got it! • Paid: $_____
Market Value: **$80**

87   #4037

Rainbow™
Chameleon • Born: 10-14-97
Issued: 1998 • Current
○ Got it! • Paid: $_____
Market Value: $_____

88   #4086

Rex™
Tyrannosaurus • Born: N/A
Issued: 1995 • Retired: 1996
○ Got it! • Paid: $_____
Market Value: **$385**

Value
Totals _____

COLLECTOR'S
VALUE GUIDE™

89   #4086

Righty™
Elephant • Born: 7-4-96
Issued: 1996 • Retired: 1997
◯ Got it! • Paid: $_____
Market Value: **$110**

90   #4014

Ringo™
Raccoon • Born: 7-14-95
Issued: 1996 • Current
◯ Got it! • Paid: $_____
Market Value. $_____

91   #4069

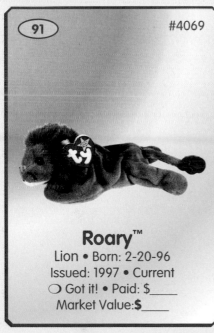

Roary™
Lion • Born: 2-20-96
Issued: 1997 • Current
◯ Got it! • Paid: $_____
Market Value:$_____

92   #4101

Rover™
Dog • Born: 5-30-96
Issued: 1996 • Current
◯ Got it! • Paid: $_____
Market Value: $_____

COLLECTOR'S
VALUE GUIDE™

Value
Totals _____

My Beanie Babies® Collection

93 #4107

Scoop™
Pelican • Born: 7-1-96
Issued: 1996 • Current
○ Got it! • Paid: $_____
Market Value: $_____

94 #4102

Scottie™
Scottish Terrier • Born: 6-15-96
Issued: 1996 • Current
○ Got it! • Paid: $_____
Market Value: $_____

95 #4029

Seamore™
Seal • Born: 12-14-96
Issued: 1994 • Retired: 1997
○ Got it! • Paid: $_____
Market Value: **$55**

96 #4080

Seaweed™
Otter • Born: 3-19-96
Issued: 1996 • Current
○ Got it! • Paid: $_____
Market Value: $_____

Value
Totals _____

COLLECTOR'S
VALUE GUIDE™

97 #4031

Slither™
Snake • Born: N/A
Issued: 1994 • Retired: 1996
○ Got it! • Paid: $____
Market Value: **$975**

98 #4115

a

b

Sly™
Fox • Born: 9-12-96
Issued: 1996 • Current
○ Got it! • Paid: $____
Market Value:
a. **White belly – $____**
b. **Brown belly – $100**

99 #4039

Smoochy™
Frog • Born: 10-1-97
Issued: 1998 • Current
○ Got it! • Paid: $____
Market Value: $____

100 #4120

Snip™
Siamese Cat • Born: 10-22-96
Issued: 1997 • Current
○ Got it! • Paid: $____
Market Value: $____

COLLECTOR'S
VALUE GUIDE™

Value
Totals _____

My Beanie Babies® Collection

101   #4002

Snort™
Bull • Born: 5-15-95
Issued: 1997 • Current
○ Got it! • Paid: $____
Market Value: $____

102   #4201

Snowball™
Snowman • Born: 12-22-96
Issued: 1997 • Retired: 1998
○ Got it! • Paid: $____
Market Value: **$75**

103   #4100

Sparky™
Dalmatian • Born: 2-27-96
Issued: 1996 • Retired: 1997
○ Got it! • Paid: $____
Market Value: **$60**

104   #4030

Speedy™
Turtle • Born: 8-14-94
Issued: 1994 • Retired: 1997
○ Got it! • Paid: $____
Market Value: **$35**

Value
Totals _____

COLLECTOR'S
VALUE GUIDE™

105   #4060

Spike™
Rhinoceros • Born: 8-13-96
Issued: 1996 • Current
○ Got it! • Paid: $____
Market Value: $____

106   #4036

Spinner™
Spider • Born: 10-28-96
Issued: 1997 • Current
○ Got it! • Paid: $____
Market Value: $____

107   #4022

Splash™
Whale • Born: 7-8-93
Issued: 1994* • Retired: 1997
○ Got it! • Paid: $____
Market Value: **$55**
* one of the "Original 9"

108   #4090

a   b

Spooky™
Ghost • Born: 10-31-95
Issued: 1995 • Retired: 1998
○ Got it! • Paid: $____
Market Value:
a. "Spooky" tag – $55
b. "Spook" tag – $150

COLLECTOR'S
VALUE GUIDE™

Value
Totals _____

109   #4000

Spot™
Dog • Born: 1-3-93
Issued: 1994* • Retired: 1997
○ Got it! • Paid: $_____
Market Value:
a. With spot on back – $40
b. Without spot – $1,300
* one of the "Original 9"

110   #4184

Spunky™
Cocker Spaniel • Born: 1-14-97
Issued: 1998 • Current
○ Got it! • Paid: $_____
Market Value: $_____

111   #4005

Squealer™
Pig • Born: 4-23-93
Issued: 1994* • Current
○ Got it! • Paid: $_____
Market Value: $_____
* one of the "Original 9"

112   #4087

Steg™
Stegosaurus • Born: N/A
Issued: 1995 • Retired: 1996
○ Got it! • Paid: $_____
Market Value: **$370**

Value
Totals _____

113   #4077

Sting™
Manta Ray • Born: 8-27-95
Issued: 1995 • Retired: 1997
○ Got it! • Paid: $____
Market Value: **$90**

114   #4017

Stinky™
Skunk • Born: 2-13-95
Issued: 1995 • Current
○ Got it! • Paid: $____
Market Value: $____

115   #4182

Stretch™
Ostrich • Born: 9-21-97
Issued: 1998 • Current
○ Got it! • Paid: $____
Market Value: $____

116   #4065

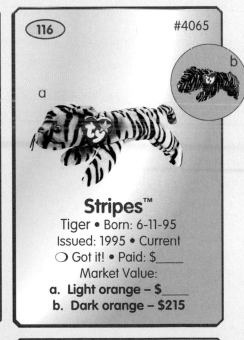

a

b

Stripes™
Tiger • Born: 6-11-95
Issued: 1995 • Current
○ Got it! • Paid: $____
Market Value:
a. **Light orange** – $____
b. **Dark orange** – **$215**

Value
Totals _____

117 #4171

Strut™
Rooster • Born: 3-8-96
Issued: 1997 • Current
○ Got it! • Paid: $____
Market Value:
a. "Strut" – $____
b. "Doodle" variation – $45

118 #4002

Tabasco™
Bull • Born: 5-15-95
Issued: 1995 • Retired: 1997
○ Got it! • Paid: $____
Market Value: **$200**

119 #4031

a

Tank™
Armadillo • Born: 2-22-95
Issued: 1996 • Retired: 1997
○ Got it! • Paid: $____
Market Value:
a. 9 plates, with shell – $55
b. 9 plates, no shell – $115
c. 7 plates, no shell – $105

120 #4050

a

b

Teddy™
Brown Bear • Born: 11-28-95
Issued: 1994 • Retired: 1997
○ Got it! • Paid: $____
Market Value:
a. New face – $60
b. Old face – $1,200

Value
Totals _____

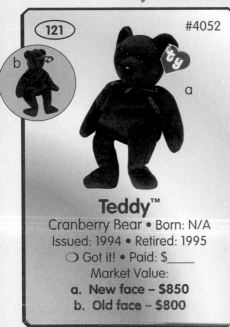

121 #4052

Teddy™
Cranberry Bear • Born: N/A
Issued: 1994 • Retired: 1995
○ Got it! • Paid: $_____
Market Value:
a. New face – $850
b. Old face – $800

122 #4057

Teddy™
Jade Bear • Born: N/A
Issued: 1994 • Retired: 1995
○ Got it! • Paid: $_____
Market Value:
a. New face – $850
b. Old face – $775

123 #4056

Teddy™
Magenta Bear • Born: N/A
Issued: 1994 • Retired: 1995
○ Got it! • Paid: $_____
Market Value:
a. New face – $850
b. Old face – $775

124 #4051

Teddy™
Teal Bear • Born: N/A
Issued: 1994 • Retired: 1995
○ Got it! • Paid: $_____
Market Value:
a. New face – $870
b. Old face – $775

COLLECTOR'S
VALUE GUIDE™

Value
Totals _____

125 #4055

b a

Teddy™
Violet Bear • Born: N/A
Issued: 1994 • Retired: 1995
○ Got it! • Paid: $____
Market Value:
a. New face – $880
b. Old face – $775

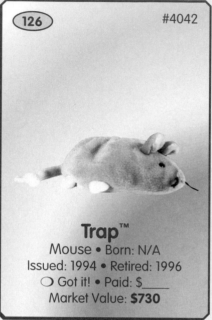

126 #4042

Trap™
Mouse • Born: N/A
Issued: 1994 • Retired: 1996
○ Got it! • Paid: $____
Market Value: **$730**

127 #4108

Tuffy™
Terrier • Born: 10-12-96
Issued: 1997 • Current
○ Got it! • Paid: $____
Market Value: $____

128 #4076

Tusk™
Walrus • Born: 9-18-95
Issued: 1995 • Retired: 1997
○ Got it! • Paid: $____
Market Value: **$70**

Value
Totals _____

COLLECTOR'S
VALUE GUIDE™

(129) #4068

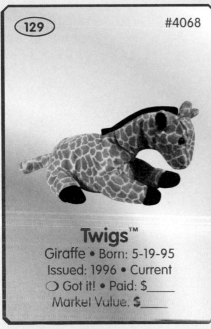

Twigs™
Giraffe • Born: 5-19-95
Issued: 1996 • Current
○ Got it! • Paid: $____
Market Value: $____

(130) #4058

Valentino™
Bear • Born: 2-14-94
Issued: 1995 • Current
○ Got it! • Paid: $____
Market Value: $____

(131) #4064

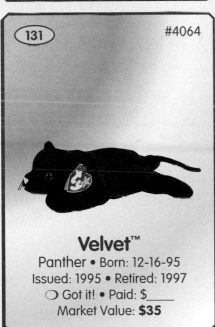

Velvet™
Panther • Born: 12-16-95
Issued: 1995 • Retired: 1997
○ Got it! • Paid: $____
Market Value: **$35**

(132) #4075

Waddle™
Penguin • Born: 12-19-95
Issued: 1995 • Current
○ Got it! • Paid: $____
Market Value: $____

Value
Totals _____

133   #4084

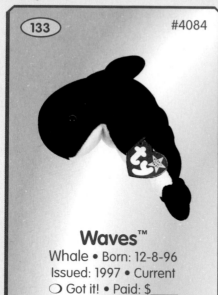

Waves™
Whale • Born: 12-8-96
Issued: 1997 • Current
○ Got it! • Paid: $_____
Market Value: $_____

134   #4041

Web™
Spider • Born: N/A
Issued: 1994 • Retired: 1996
○ Got it! • Paid: $_____
Market Value: **$700**

135   #4013

Weenie™
Dog • Born: 7-20-95
Issued: 1996 • Current
○ Got it! • Paid: $_____
Market Value: $_____

136   #4103

Wrinkles™
Dog • Born: 5-1-96
Issued: 1996 • Current
○ Got it! • Paid: $_____
Market Value: $_____

Value
Totals _____

COLLECTOR'S
VALUE GUIDE™

137 #4063

Ziggy™
Zebra • Born: 12-24-95
Issued: 1995 • Current
○ Got it! • Paid: $____
Market Value: $____

138 #4004

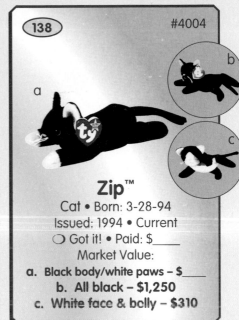
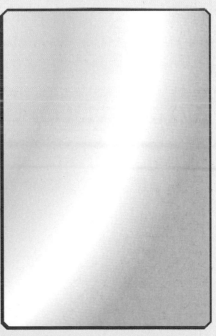

a

b

c

Zip™
Cat • Born: 3-28-94
Issued: 1994 • Current
○ Got it! • Paid: $____
Market Value:
a. **Black body/white paws – $____**
b. **All black – $1,250**
c. **White face & belly – $310**

COLLECTOR'S
VALUE GUIDE™

Value
Totals ____

My Teenie Beanie Babies™ Collection

TB1
4th Release

Chocolate™
Moose • Size: 5-1/2"
Issued & Retired: April 1997
○ Got it! • Paid: $_____
Market Value: **$9**

TB2
3rd Release

Chops™
Lamb • Size: 5"
Issued & Retired: April 1997
○ Got it! • Paid: $_____
Market Value: **$9**

TB3
5th Release

Goldie™
Goldfish • Size: 4-1/2"
Issued & Retired: April 1997
○ Got it! • Paid: $_____
Market Value: **$9**

TB4
10th Release

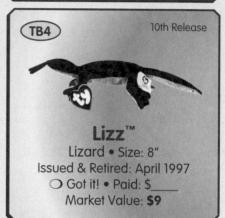

Lizz™
Lizard • Size: 8"
Issued & Retired: April 1997
○ Got it! • Paid: $_____
Market Value: **$9**

TB5
1st Release

Patti™
Platypus • Size: 5-1/2"
Issued & Retired: April 1997
m Got it! • Paid: $_____
Market Value: **$12**

TB6
2nd Release

Pinky™
Flamingo • Size: 7"
Issued & Retired: April 1997
m Got it! • Paid: $_____
Market Value: **$15**

Value
Totals _____

COLLECTOR'S
VALUE GUIDE™

My Teenie Beanie Babies™ Collection

TB7 · 9th Release

Quacks™
Duck • Size: 3-1/2"
Issued & Retired: April 1997
○ Got it! • Paid: $____
Market Value: **$9**

TB8 · 7th Release

Seamore™
Seal • Size: 4-1/2"
Issued & Retired: April 1997
○ Got it! • Paid: $____
Market Value: **$9**

TB9 · 8th Release

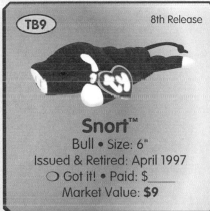

Snort™
Bull • Size: 6"
Issued & Retired: April 1997
○ Got it! • Paid: $____
Market Value: **$9**

TB10 · 6th Release

Speedy™
Turtle • Size: 4"
Issued & Retired: April 1997
○ Got it! • Paid: $____
Market Value: **$9**

COLLECTOR'S ™
VALUE GUIDE™

Value
Totals _____

My Pillow Pals™ Collection

PP1   #3008

Ba Ba™
Lamb • Size: 15"
Issued: 1997 • Current
○ Got it! • Paid: $_____
Market Value: $_____

PP2   #3018

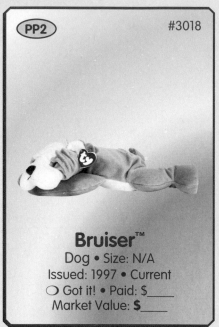

Bruiser™
Dog • Size: N/A
Issued: 1997 • Current
○ Got it! • Paid: $_____
Market Value: $_____

PP3   #3010

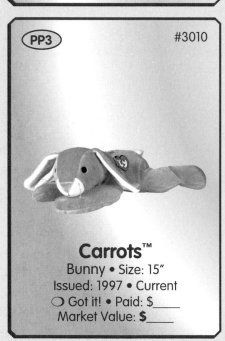

Carrots™
Bunny • Size: 15"
Issued: 1997 • Current
○ Got it! • Paid: $_____
Market Value: $_____

PP4   #3020

Clover™
Rabbit• Size: 15"
Issued: 1998 • Current
○ Got it! • Paid: $_____
Market Value: $_____

Value
Totals _____

COLLECTOR'S
VALUE GUIDE™

PP5 #3022

Foxy™
Fox • Size: 19"
Issued: 1998 • Current
○ Got it! • Paid: $____
Market Value: $____

PP6 #3025

Glide™
Porpoise• Size: 14"
Issued: 1998 • Current
○ Got it! • Paid: $____
Market Value: $____

PP7 #3002

Huggy™
Bear • Size: 15"
Issued: 1995 • Retired: 1998
○ Got it! • Paid: $____
Market Value: **N/E**

PP8 #3011

Meow™
Cat • Size: 15"
Issued: 1997 • Current
○ Got it! • Paid: $____
Market Value:
a. tan – $____
b. gray – N/E

COLLECTOR'S
VALUE GUIDE™

Value
Totals _____

My Pillow Pals™ Collection

PP9   #3004

Moo™
Cow • Size: 15"
Issued: 1995 • Current
○ Got it! • Paid: $____
Market Value: $____

PP10   #3005

Oink™
Pig • Size: 15"
Issued: 1995 • Current
○ Got it! • Paid: $____
Market Value: $____

PP11   #3016

Purr™
Tiger • Size: 15"
Issued: 1997 • Current
○ Got it! • Paid: $____
Market Value: $____

PP12   #3021

Red™
Bull • Size: 15"
Issued: 1998 • Current
○ Got it! • Paid: $____
Market Value: $____

Value
Totals _____

COLLECTOR'S
VALUE GUIDE™

PP13 #3006

Ribbit™
Frog • Size: 14"
Issued: 1995 • Out of Production
○ Got it! • Paid: $_____
Market Value: **N/E**

PP14 #3009

Ribbit™
Frog • Size: 14"
Issued: 1997 • Current
○ Got it! • Paid: $_____
Market Value: **$_____**

PP15 #3007

Snap™
Turtle • Size: 14"
Issued: 1995 • Out of Production
○ Got it! • Paid: $_____
Market Value: **N/E**

PP16 #3015

Snap™
Turtle • Size: 14"
Issued: 1997 • Current
○ Got it! • Paid: $_____
Market Value: **$_____**

COLLECTOR'S
VALUE GUIDE™

Value
Totals _____

My Pillow Pals™ Collection

PP17   #3001

Snuggy™
Bear • Size: 15"
Issued: 1995 • Retired: 1998
○ Got it! • Paid: $_____
Market Value: **N/E**

PP18   #3017

Speckles™
Leopard • Size: N/A
Issued: 1997 • Current
○ Got it! • Paid: $_____
Market Value: $_____

PP19   #3019

Spotty™
Dalmatian • Size: 15"
Issued: 1998 • Current
○ Got it! • Paid: $_____
Market Value: $_____

PP20   #3013

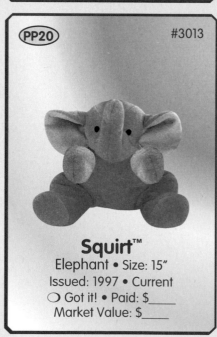

Squirt™
Elephant • Size: 15"
Issued: 1997 • Current
○ Got it! • Paid: $_____
Market Value: $_____

Value
Totals _____

COLLECTOR'S
VALUE GUIDE™

PP21   #3023

Swinger™
Monkey • Size: 15"
Issued: 1998 • Current
○ Got it! • Paid: $____
Market Value: $____

PP22   #3024

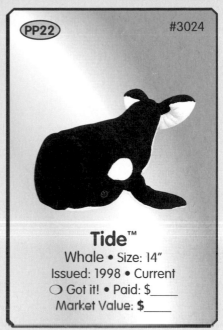

Tide™
Whale • Size: 14"
Issued: 1998 • Current
○ Got it! • Paid: $____
Market Value: $____

PP23   #3012

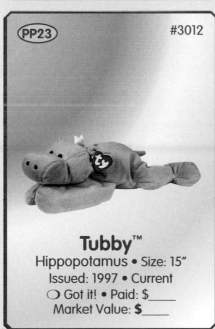

Tubby™
Hippopotamus • Size: 15"
Issued: 1997 • Current
○ Got it! • Paid: $____
Market Value: $____

PP24   #3003

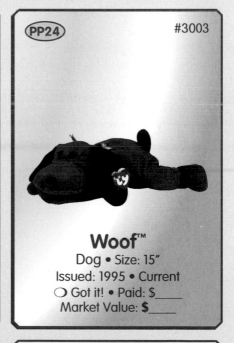

Woof™
Dog • Size: 15"
Issued: 1995 • Current
○ Got it! • Paid: $____
Market Value: $____

COLLECTOR'S
VALUE GUIDE™

Value
Totals _____

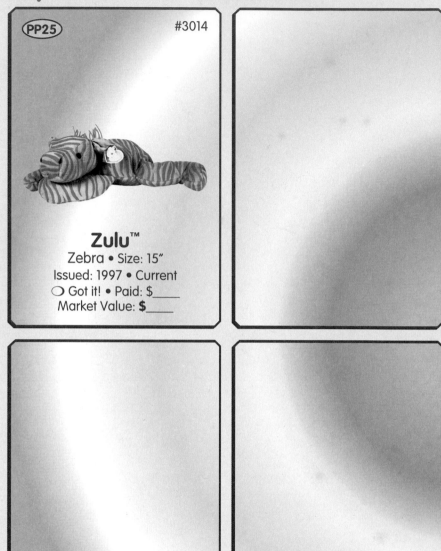

PP25   #3014

Zulu™
Zebra • Size: 15"
Issued: 1997 • Current
◯ Got it! • Paid: $____
Market Value: $____

Value
Totals _____

Name	Description	Value
1.		
2.		
3.		
4.		
5.		
6.		
7.		
8.		
9.		
10.		
11.		
12.		
13.		
14.		
15.		
16.		

COLLECTOR'S
VALUE GUIDE™

Value
Totals _____

Total Value Of My Collection

Value Totals

Page 19

Page 20

Page 21

Page 22

Page 23

Page 24

Page 25

Page 26

Page 27

Page 28

Page 29

Page 30

Page 31

Page 32

Page 33

Page 34

Page 35

Page 36

Page 37

Page 38

Page 39

Page 40

Page 41

Subtotal

Value Totals

Page 42

Page 43

Page 44

Page 45

Page 46

Page 47

Page 48

Page 49

Page 50

Page 51

Page 52

Page 53

Page 54

Page 55

Page 56

Page 57

Page 58

Page 59

Page 60

Page 61

Page 62

Page 63

Subtotal

GRAND TOTAL _____

COLLECTOR'S
VALUE GUIDE™

*W*hen Ty created the first Beanie Babies less than five years ago, no one was prepared for what lay ahead. Interest in Beanie Babies slowly began to build as more people discovered the adorable little critters. To their surprise, gift and toy industry retailers began to notice that people were "collecting" Beanie Babies.

Beanie Babies have struck a chord with many collectors for two big reasons. First, the plush toys are very affordable which means it's easy to buy multiple Beanie Babies on one shopping excursion. Secondly, the pursuit of Beanies is fun. Collectors enjoy the challenge of hunting from store to store for hard-to-find Beanies.

As the Beanie Babies Collection grew in popularity, the demand quickly outstripped the supply available in stores. As seemingly every kid (and many adults!) in America begged for more Beanie Babies, many people turned to the secondary market to buy their "must-haves" at prices higher than retail.

THE SECONDARY MARKET BOOM

The secondary marketplace for Beanie Babies has become HUGE! Pieces are listed for sale all over the Internet and die-hard collectors are likely to find collector shows in their area nearly every weekend. The older, "retired" Beanie Babies command top dollar, as do the earlier variations of existing pieces (see *Variations* section on page 68). When a piece is retired, it is removed from production by Ty and is no longer available in retail stores once the existing stock runs out. As is typical with most collectibles, demand for the piece increases as it becomes more scarce. These factors help trigger an increase in the piece's value on the secondary market.

Because the Beanie craze took a while to catch on, many pieces came and went before people's interest in them was piqued. Some pieces had a relatively short shelf life, as they were quickly retired. Others did not fare well when introduced to the public, such as "Bronty" the brontosaurus, who was hampered by weak stitching. As a result, there are a lot fewer "Bronty" Beanies in circulation than were actually produced.

Perhaps the most unique aspect of the Beanie Babies secondary market is the tremendous demand for new introductions. Anticipating a shortage or a quick retirement (such as "1997 Teddy" and "Snowball," which were only available for two months), collectors will often pay inflated prices for new Beanie Babies, despite the fact that, at least theoretically, the pieces are available in retail stores for under $10. The December 1997 release of "Princess," a teddy which benefits the Diana, Princess of Wales Memorial Fund, created an unparalleled demand as initially only a dozen pieces were allotted to each retail outlet.

Some "Princess" Beanie Babies fetched hundreds of dollars on the secondary market in December of 1997.

The secondary market activity on currently available Beanie Babies is a great source of excitement for Beanie collectors. A word of advice to desperate collectors – be patient in your own pursuit of current Beanie Babies. One person may charge you $20 while another vendor will only charge you $10. The old adage is true: It pays to shop around.

WHERE IS THE SECONDARY MARKET?

So, how can you find the secondary market? Conventional methods include retail stores, swap-and-sell meets and classified ads. Contact retailers to find out if they have older Beanies for sale, or if they would like to buy Beanies that you have for sale. Ask your retailer about swap-and-sell meets in the area. Another route to the secondary marketplace is through classified ads in the "antiques/collectibles" section in your local newspaper.

If you have access to a computer, you can contact other Beanie Babies collectors directly. You'll be amazed at all the Beanie Babies information you'll find when you surf the Web. Everything you've ever wanted to know about these huggable little creatures can be found on the Internet, from general information to discussions over details of individual Beanie Babies. The Beanie Babies market fluctuates rapidly, so astute shoppers can explore the Web to see the latest prices that Beanies are selling for and make sure they're getting a good deal. Collectors can buy, sell and trade through e-mail or by entering a "swap-and-sell" board. No doubt about it, websurfing is a lot of fun. A word of caution, though – do not give out any personal information about yourself on the Internet. And children should let their parents know when they are going on-line.

With this wealth of information comes a wealth of options. Look around before you commit to buying a piece. If you ever get too frustrated in the midst of your Beanie hunt, remember, it's only a little stuffed animal! Ultimately, the value will be what a buyer is willing to spend.

VARIATIONS

Birthdate Variation

Freckles™ style 4066
DATE OF BIRTH: 6 - 3 - 96
From the trees he hunts prey
In the night and in the day
He's the king of camouflage
Look real close, he's no mirage!
Visit our web page!!!
http://www.ty.com

Freckles™ style 4066
DATE OF BIRTH: 7 - 28 - 96
From the trees he hunts prey
In the night and in the day
He's the king of camouflage
Look real close, he's no mirage!
Visit our web page!!!
http://www.ty.com

Poem Variation

Tusk™ style 4076
DATE OF BIRTH: 9 - 18 - 95
Tusk brushes his teeth everyday
To keep them shiny, it's the only way
Teeth are special, so you must try
To sparkle when you say 'Hi'!
Visit our web page!!!
http://www.ty.com

Tusk™ style 4076
DATE OF BIRTH: 9 - 18 - 95
Tusk brushes his teeth everyday
To keep them shiny, it's the only way
Teeth are special, so you must try
And they will sparkle when
You say "Hi"!
Visit our web page!!!
http://www.ty.com

*O*ne of the interesting "side effects" of the Beanie craze is the avid collectors' search for variations. As Beanie Babies started to become "collectible," people began to notice differences among the Beanies that they owned. They began to share this information with other collectors by word-of-mouth and, especially, on the Internet. Soon, people everywhere were whispering about the mysterious dark blue elephant "Peanut" and the wingless duck "Quackers."

The search for Beanie variations has helped fuel the already-bustling secondary market activity for Beanie Babies. Some variations are now highly-coveted by collectors and can be sold for thousands of dollars. Other variations are mere curiosities and don't affect the secondary market value.

The Beanie variations that are most significant to avid collectors are color changes, name changes and physical design changes. Some collectors have picked up on the various changes in the Ty hang tags and tush tags attached to the Beanies and seek out animals with "older" tags (see page 75). There are also a fair number of slight tag variations affecting the Beanie's name ("Punchers" instead of "Pinchers," "Tuck" instead of "Tusk," etc.) and other tag information, such as the birthdates and poems.

While some of these variations do command top dollar, it is up to each individual collector to decide for themself which Beanie Babies are really worth the pursuit. Beware of variations that may be the result of someone's creative handiwork. After all, you don't want to find out that the seven-legged Inky that you've just paid "an arm and a leg" for has undergone an operation and has the scars to show for it!

On these next few pages are some of the common, and not-so-common, variations out there.

COLOR CHANGES

Digger . . . Although she was initially orange, after about six months in the sun, this crab's shell changed to a lovely red color.

Happy . . . Originally the everyday gray kind of hippopotamus, "Happy" was so delighted that he transcended his original shade of pale and bloomed into a cheery lavender color. The lavender version of "Happy" is still current.

Inky . . . The same sun that turned "Digger" red gave the fair-skinned octopus, "Inky" a sunburn. Originally tan, "Inky" has transformed into a bright pink sea creature.

Lizzy . . . Initially tie-dyed in a rainbow of colors, "Lizzy" the lizard, finally grew up and shifted, chameleon-like, into a fashionable suit. She now wears, with confidence, a navy blue coat with black spots over a yellow belly with orange spots.

Patti . . . "Patti" the platypus has been found in shades of purple and magenta. Other slight color variations of "Patti" have been reported.

Peanut . . . "Peanut" was mistakenly produced for one month in a rich dark blue before production was stopped and a color more appropriate for an elephant was used. "Peanut" is now a light blue.

NAME CHANGES

Brownie/Cubbie . . . This bear was originally released as "Brownie," but the name was later changed to "Cubbie." The only way to tell them apart is by reading their tags.

Doodle/Strut . . . This rooster was introduced as "Doodle," but the name was changed – rumor has it – because of a copyright conflict. But that's okay, because "Strut" quickly shuffled in to replace him.

Maple . . . Just as the time came for this cuddly white Canadian bear to make his debut to the public, a last-minute name change left him with his new moniker, "Maple," on his hang tag, while his old name, "Pride," was left on the tush tag.

Nana/Bongo . . . This monkey was first introduced as "Nana," a brown monkey with a brown tail. The monkey's name was soon changed to "Bongo," and the tail changed back and forth between brown and tan several times.

PHYSICAL DESIGN CHANGES

Derby . . . This horse's mane has appeared in two styles. "Derby" first appeared with a mane and a tail made from fine yarn, and later came back with coarse yarn locks. More recently, "Derby" has started to arrive in stores with a white spot on his forehead.

Inch . . . At first, this inchworm could be found measuring the marigolds with perky little black felt antennae. This was later changed, and "Inch" appeared sporting new black yarn antennae.

Lucky . . . "Lucky" flew into the world with seven spots made of felt and glued onto her ladybug shell. With all the flying around she has to do, "Lucky" began appearing with dots that were sewn on, first with a total of 21 dots and now 11 dots.

Magic . . . This dragon originally had iridescent wings stitched with pale pink thread. The thread was changed to hot pink, and then reverted to pale pink once again.

Mystic . . . "Mystic" the unicorn originally sported a mane and tail cut from fine yarn. The mane and tail were later changed to coarse yarn. The most recent incarnation features "Mystic" wearing an iridescent horn which is about 3/4" longer than her original tan horn.

Nip . . . "Nip" has already used up three of his nine lives. Originally gold with a white face and belly, she later changed to a solid gold feline, then a gold kitty with white paws. In the two later versions, a gold ring can be seen around his eyes.

Quackers . . . Someone forgot to include wings when designing "Quackers" and the poor duck was looking a little lost without them. Now that he's been redesigned with wings, he can soar with the eagles if he wants to!

Sly . . . Tired of being the number one suspect, "Sly" the fox has made a deliberate attempt to be more visible. His coat has changed from brown with a patch of white underneath his chin, to brown with a white belly and chin.

Spooky . . . "Spooky," which was named "Spook" on some tags, has three facial variations: a full smile, a half-smile and a v-shaped smile.

Spot . . . The first version of this playful little pup named "Spot" didn't have a spot on his back. Desiring to be truer to his name, "Spot" barked at all hours of the night until Ty agreed to add a spot and restore order to the world.

Stripes . . . "Stripes" first appeared with a dark orange and black tiger-striped coat. A later version of this wildcat featured a lighter orange and black striped coat, with the stripes farther apart. "Stripes" has also been found with a fuzzy belly in the darker version.

Tank . . . The first version introduced "Tank" with seven plates and small ears that were sewn into the seams on the sides of his face. The second time around, the armadillo sported nine plates. Today, "Tank" has the same nine plate shell, with seams sewn at the bottom to more clearly define it, and perky little ears sticking up out of the top of his head.

Teddy . . . All of the bears named "Teddy" – colored brown, cranberry, jade, magenta, teal and violet – underwent face lifts. Characteristics of the "old face" are a pointed snout and eyes set far apart on the side of the face. The "new face" featured eyes closer together on the front of the face and a larger, rounded nose. Both versions of these bears are highly coveted by collectors.

Zip . . . "Zip" first appeared as a black kitty with white fur on the chin and the belly. For a short time, he appeared as an all-black cat and later showed up as a black cat with white front paws. The last two versions of "Zip" also featured green circles around the eyes.

*W*hen Beanie Babies first arrived on the retail scene in 1994, no one knew that the simple heart-shaped hang tags (also known as "heart tags" or "swing tags") and the "tush" tags attached to the seam would become factors in the future value of their Beanies. Certainly, most early purchasers of Beanie Babies removed and discarded the tags without a moment's hesitation. Today, many collectors consider a "tag-less" Beanie to be worth about half the secondary market value of an identical Beanie with its tags intact. The following are the four "generations" of Ty hang tags produced to date.

Hang Tags

1st

The first of the Ty hang tags was a single heart with the original thin Ty log on the front and the style number, name and Ty information on the back.

The second version of the tag had the same Ty logo as the first, but was issued in a folded "booklet" format consisting of two attached hearts. In addition to the style number, name and Ty information, this tag introduced the "To:/From:" section for gift givers.

2nd

The third generation of tags pictured an "inflated" Ty logo and featured the same inside information as the previous version of the tag.

The fourth version of the tag also featured the wider lettering on the Ty logo, with the addition of a yellow star identifying the toy as an "Original Beanie Baby." This was the first tag to include the birthdate and poem, as well as the Ty website address.

3rd

4th

As the 1998 releases arrive in stores, collectors will notice some font changes on the inside of the tag, as well as changes in the registered trademark symbol next to "Beanie Babies." Will this become known as the "fifth generation" tag? We'll have to wait and see.

Tush Tags

1st

2nd

3rd

4th

Tush tags, also known as "body tags," are sewn into a seam on each Beanie. Tush tags have also been identified by Beanie collectors as having several generations.

The first generation tush tag was printed in black ink. This tag had the name of the country where it was made (Korea or China), but did not include the name of the Beanie.

The second generation tush tag was printed in red ink and featured the Ty logo for the first time. The Beanie's name still did not appear.

The third tush tag was the first to include the Beanie's name. This version, also in red ink, featured a smaller Ty logo below the words "The Beanie Babies Collection™."

In 1997, the fourth generation of the tag was introduced. The only difference between tags from the third and fourth generations is the small red star next to the Ty logo. Clear stickers with a star were added to some tush tags that had already been manufactured.

By late 1997, revised tush tags appeared with the registered trademark symbol (®) next to "Beanie Babies" and the trademark symbol (™) next to the Beanie's name. Some collectors are considering this version a possible "fifth generation" tush tag.

Different combinations of hang and tush tags yield different values on the secondary market. For instance, some collectors feel that a "Flash" with the first generation hang tag is worth more than one with a third generation hang tag because it is technically "older." It's up to each individual collector to decide whether to pay more for a Beanie with an older tag.

Since early 1996, Ty has included poems on the Beanie Babies' hang tags. Many tags have variations in spelling, punctuation or even wording! See if your Beanie Babies' poems match these official Ty poems. Beanies which stopped production prior to 1996 were never assigned a poem. Have some fun and create your own! (Note: Ty had not confirmed the 1998 Beanie poems by press time.)

1997 Teddy™

Beanie Babies are special no doubt
All filled with love – inside and out
Wishes for fun times filled with joy
Ty's holiday teddy is a magical toy!

Ally™

When Ally gets out of classes
He wears a hat and dark glasses
He plays bass in a street band
He's the coolest gator in the land!

Baldy™

Hair on his head is quite scant
We suggest Baldy get a transplant
Watching over the land of the free
Hair in his eyes would make it hard to see!

Batty™

Bats may make some people jitter
Please don't be scared of this critter
If you're lonely or have nothing to do
This Beanie Baby would love to hug you!

Bernie™

This little dog can't wait to grow
To rescue people lost in the snow
Don't let him out – keep him on your shelf
He doesn't know how to rescue himself!

Bessie™

Bessie the cow likes to dance and sing
Because music is her favorite thing
Every night when you are counting sheep
She'll sing you a song to help you sleep!

Blackie™

Living in a national park
He only played after dark
Then he met his friend Cubbie
Now they play when it's sunny!

Blizzard™

In the mountains, where it's snowy and cold
Lives a beautiful tiger, I've been told
Black and white, she's hard to compare
Of all the tigers, she is most rare!

Bones™

Bones is a dog that loves to chew
Chairs and tables and a smelly old shoe
"You're so destructive" all would shout
But that all stopped, when his teeth
Fell out!

Bongo™

Bongo the monkey lives in a tree
The happiest monkey you'll ever see
In his spare time he plays the guitar
One of these days he will be a big star!

Britannia™

Poem Unavailable

_____
_____
_____
_____

Bronty™

No Poem

_____
_____
_____

Beanie Babies® Poems

Brownie™

No Poem
_____
_____
_____
_____

Chocolate™

Licorice, gum and peppermint candy
This moose always has these handy
There is one more thing he likes to eat
Can you guess his favorite sweet?

Bruno™

Bruno the dog thinks he's a brute
But all the other Beanies think he's cute
He growls at his tail and runs in a ring
And everyone says, "Oh, how darling!"

Chops™

Chops is a little lamb
This lamb you'll surely know
Because every path that you may take
This lamb is sure to go!

Bubbles™

All day long Bubbles likes to swim
She never gets tired of flapping her fins
Bubbles lived in a sea of blue
Now she is ready to come home with you!

Claude™

Claude the crab paints by the sea
A famous artist he hopes to be
But the tide came in and his paints fell
Now his art is on his shell!

Bucky™

Bucky's teeth are as shiny as can be
Often used for cutting trees
He hides in his dam night and day
Maybe for you he will come out and play!

Congo™

Black as the night and fierce is he
On the ground or in a tree
Strong and mighty as the Congo
He's related to our Bongo!

Bumble™
Bumble the bee will not sting you
It is only love that this bee will bring you
So don't be afraid to give this bee a hug
Because Bumble the bee is a love-bug.

Coral™

Coral is beautiful, as you know
Made of colors in the rainbow
Whether it's pink, yellow or blue
These colors were chosen just for you!

Caw™

No Poem
_____
_____
_____
_____

Crunch™

What's for breakfast? What's for lunch?
Yum! Delicious! Munch, munch, munch!
He's eating everything by the bunch
That's the reason we named him Crunch!

Chilly™
No Poem
_____
_____
_____
_____

Cubbie™

Cubbie used to eat crackers and honey
And what happened to him was funny
He was stung by fourteen bees
Now Cubbie eats broccoli and cheese!

Chip™

Black and gold, brown and white
The shades of her coat are quite a sight
At mixing her colors she was a master
On anyone else it would be a disaster!

Curly™
A bear so cute with hair that's Curly
You will love and want him surely
To this bear always be true
He will be a friend to you!

BEANIE BABIES® POEMS

Daisy™

Daisy drinks milk each night
So her coat is shiny and bright
Milk is good for your hair and skin
What a way for your day to begin!

Flash™

You know dolphins are a smart breed
Our friend Flash knows how to read
Splash the whale is the one who taught her
Although reading is difficult under the water!

Derby™

All the other horses used to tattle
Because Derby never wore his saddle
He left the stables, and the horses too
Just so Derby can be with you!

Fleece™

Fleece would like to sing a lullaby
But please be patient, she's rather shy
When you sleep, keep her by your ear
Her song will leave you nothing to fear.

Digger™

Digging in the sand and walking sideways
That's how Digger spends her days
Hard on the outside but sweet deep inside
Basking in the sun and riding the tide!

Flip™

Flip the cat is an acrobat
She loves playing on her mat
This cat flips with such grace and flair
She can somersault in mid air!

Doby™

This dog is little but he has might
Keep him close when you sleep at night
He lays around with nothing to do
Until he sees it's time to protect you!

Floppity™

Floppity hops from here to there
Searching for eggs without a care
Lavender coat from head to toe
All dressed up and nowhere to go!

Doodle™

Listen closely to "cock-a-doodle-doo"
What's the rooster saying to you?
Hurry, wake up sleepy head
We have lots to do, get out of bed!

Flutter™

No Poem
_____
_____
_____
_____

Dotty™

The Beanies all thought it was a big joke
While writing her tag, their ink pen broke
She got in the way, and got all spotty
So now the Beanies call her Dotty!

Freckles™

From the trees he hunts prey
In the night and in the day
He's the king of camouflage
Look real close, he's no mirage!

Ears™

He's been eating carrots so long
Didn't understand what was wrong
Couldn't see the board during classes
Until the doctor gave him glasses!

Garcia™

The Beanies use to follow him around
Because Garcia traveled from town to town
He's pretty popular as you can see
Some even say he's legendary!

Echo™

Echo the dolphin lives in the sea
Playing with her friends, like you and me
Through the waves she echoes the sound
"I'm so glad to have you around!"

Gobbles™

Gobbles the turkey loves to eat
Once a year she has a feast
I have a secret I'd like to divulge
If she eats too much her tummy will bulge!

Beanie Babies® Poems

Goldie™

She's got rhythm, she's got soul
What more to like in a fish bowl?
Through sound waves Goldie swam
Because this goldfish likes to jam!

Humphrey™

No Poem

_____
_____
_____
_____

Gracie™

As a duckling, she was confused,
Birds on the lake were quite amused.
Poking fun until she would cry,
Now the most beautiful swan at Ty!

Iggy™

Sitting on a rock, basking in the sun
Is this iguana's idea of fun
Towel and glasses, book and beach chair
His life is so perfect without a care!

Grunt™

Some Beanies think Grunt is tough
No surprise, he's scary enough
But if you take him home you'll see
Grunt is the sweetest Beanie Baby!

Inch™

Inch the worm is a friend of mine
He goes so slow all the time
Inching around from here to there
Traveling the world without a care!

Happy™

Happy the Hippo loves to wade
In the river and in the shade
When Happy shoots water out of his snout
You know he's happy without a doubt!

Inky™

Inky's head is big and round
As he swims he makes no sound
If you need a hand, don't hesitate
Inky can help because he has eight!

Hippity™

Hippity is a cute little bunny
Dressed in green, he looks quite funny
Twitching his nose in the air
Sniffing a flower here and there!

Jolly™

Jolly the walrus is not very serious
He laughs and laughs until he's delirious
He often reminds me of my dad
Always happy, never sad!

Hissy™

Curled and coiled and ready to play
He waits for you patiently every day
He'll keep his best friend, but not his skin
And stay with you through thick and thin.

Kiwi™

Kiwi waits for the April showers
Watching a garden bloom with flowers
There trees grow with fruit that's sweet
I'm sure you'll guess his favorite treat!

Hoot™

Late to bed, late to rise
Nevertheless, Hoot's quite wise
Studies by candlelight, nothing new
Like a president, do you know Whooo?

Lefty™

Donkeys to the left, elephants to the right
Often seems like a crazy sight
This whole game seems very funny
Until you realize they're spending
Your money!

Hoppity™

Hopscotch is what she likes to play
If you don't join in, she'll hop away
So play a game if you have the time,
She likes to play, rain or shine!

Legs™

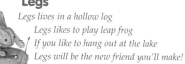

Legs lives in a hollow log
Legs likes to play leap frog
If you like to hang out at the lake
Legs will be the new friend you'll make!

Trying to keep track of my collection used to drive me batty – until I got this free pocket planner!

I really want a "Princess," but even I haven't been able to "Digger" up!

THE COLLECTOR'S POCKET PLANNER™

Detach, fold, insert in this vinyl sleeve and you'll have your handy pocket planner in a flash!

When I see a Beanie I like, I pounce on it!

Tear here, then fold to create your very own pocket planner:

Winter 1998 Edition

The Collector's
Pocket Planner™

Ty®'s Beanie Babies™

Collector's Name

$2.95

A Personal Checklist

My Collection ④

Want it	Got it!	
○	○	Scottie™, black Scottish Terrier
○	○	Seamore™, white seal
○	○	Seaweed™, brown otter
○	○	Slither™, brown/yellow snake
○	○	Sly™, brown fox †
○	○	Smoochy™, green/yellow frog
○	○	Snip™, cream/brown cat
○	○	Snort™, red bull
○	○	Snowball™, white snowman
○	○	Sparky™, black/white dalmatian
○	○	Speedy™, green turtle
○	○	Spike™, gray rhinoceros
○	○	Spinner™, black/orange spider
○	○	Splash™, black/white orca whale
○	○	Spooky™, white ghost †
○	○	Spot™, black/white dog †
○	○	Spunky™, brown cocker spaniel
○	○	Squealer™, pink pig
○	○	Steg™, tie-dye stegosaurus
○	○	Sting™, blue/green tie-dye manta ray
○	○	Stinky™, black/white skunk
○	○	Stretch™, brown/white ostrich
○	○	Stripes™, black/orange tiger †
○	○	Strut™, tie-dye rooster †
○	○	Tabasco™, red bull
○	○	Tank™, gray armadillo †
○	○	Teddy™, brown bear †
○	○	Teddy™, cranberry bear †
○	○	Teddy™, jade bear †
○	○	Teddy™, magenta bear †
○	○	Teddy™, teal bear †
○	○	Teddy™, violet bear †

My Collection ⑤

Want it	Got it!	
○	○	Trap™, gray mouse
○	○	Tuffy™, brown terrier
○	○	Tusk™, brown walrus
○	○	Twigs™, orange giraffe
○	○	Valentino™, white bear with heart
○	○	Velvet™, black panther
○	○	Waddle™, black/white penguin
○	○	Waves™, black/white orca whale
○	○	Web™, black spider
○	○	Weenie™, brown dachshund
○	○	Wrinkles™, brown/white bulldog
○	○	Ziggy™, black/white zebra
○	○	Zip™, black cat †

My Teenie Collection

Want it	Got it!	
○	○	Chocolate™, brown moose
○	○	Chops™, white lamb
○	○	Goldie™, orange goldfish
○	○	Lizz™, multi-color lizard
○	○	Patti™, purple platypus
○	○	Pinky™, pink flamingo
○	○	Quacks™, yellow duck
○	○	Seamore™, white seal
○	○	Snort™, red bull
○	○	Speedy™, green turtle

Copyright © 1998 by Collectors Publishing Co., Inc.
598 Pomeroy Avenue, Meriden, CT 06450

Visit us on the web @ www.collectorspub.com

- ○ ○ 1997 Teddy™, brown holiday bear
- ○ ○ Ally™, green alligator
- ○ ○ Baldy™, brown/white eagle
- ○ ○ Batty™, pink bat
- ○ ○ Bernie™, brown St. Bernard
- ○ ○ Bessie™, brown/white cow
- ○ ○ Blackie™, black bear
- ○ ○ Blizzard™, white/black tiger
- ○ ○ Bones™, brown dog
- ○ ○ Bongo™, brown monkey †
- ○ ○ Britannia™, brown bear
- ○ ○ Bronty™, blue tie-dye brontosaurus
- ○ ○ Brownie™, brown bear
- ○ ○ Bruno™, brown/white terrier
- ○ ○ Bubbles™, black/yellow bee
- ○ ○ Bucky™, brown beaver
- ○ ○ Bumble™, black/yellow bee
- ○ ○ Caw™, black crow
- ○ ○ Chilly™, white polar bear
- ○ ○ Chip™, black/orange/white cat
- ○ ○ Chocolate™, brown moose
- ○ ○ Chops™, white lamb
- ○ ○ Claude™, tie-dye crab
- ○ ○ Congo™, black gorilla
- ○ ○ Coral™, tie-dye tropical fish
- ○ ○ Crunch™, gray shark
- ○ ○ Cubbie™, brown bear †
- ○ ○ Curly™, brown bear
- ○ ○ Daisy™, black/white cow

† for variations of this piece, see Value Guide
retired and out of production pieces
listed in red type

- ○ ○ Derby™, brown horse †
- ○ ○ Digger™, red crab †
- ○ ○ Doby™, black/brown doberman
- ○ ○ Doodle™, tie-dye rooster
- ○ ○ Dotty™, black/white dalmatian
- ○ ○ Ears™, brown bunny
- ○ ○ Echo™, gray/white dolphin
- ○ ○ Flash™, gray dolphin
- ○ ○ Fleece™, white lamb
- ○ ○ Flip™, white cat
- ○ ○ Floppity™, lavender bunny
- ○ ○ Flutter™, tie-dye butterfly
- ○ ○ Freckles™, white/orange leopard
- ○ ○ Garcia™, tie-dye bear
- ○ ○ Goldie™, orange goldfish
- ○ ○ Gobbles™, brown/red turkey
- ○ ○ Gracie™, white swan
- ○ ○ Grunt™, red razorback
- ○ ○ Happy™, lavender hippo †
- ○ ○ Hippity™, mint green bunny
- ○ ○ Hissy™, gray/yellow snake
- ○ ○ Hoot™, brown owl
- ○ ○ Hoppity™, pink bunny
- ○ ○ Humphrey™, brown camel
- ○ ○ Iggy™, grey iguana
- ○ ○ Inch™, multi-color worm †
- ○ ○ Inky™, pink octopus †
- ○ ○ Jolly™, brown walrus
- ○ ○ Kiwi™, multi-color toucan
- ○ ○ Lefty™, blue donkey with U.S. flag
- ○ ○ Legs™, green frog
- ○ ○ Liberty™, white bear with U.S. flag

- ○ ○ Lizzy™, multi-color lizard †
- ○ ○ Lucky™, red ladybug †
- ○ ○ Magic™, white dragon †
- ○ ○ Manny™, gray manatee
- ○ ○ Maple™, white bear w/ Canadian flag †
- ○ ○ Mel™, gray/white koala
- ○ ○ Mystic™, white unicorn †
- ○ ○ Nana™, brown monkey
- ○ ○ Nanook™, gray/white husky
- ○ ○ Nip™, gold cat †
- ○ ○ Nuts™, brown squirrel
- ○ ○ Patti™, purple platypus †
- ○ ○ Peace™, tie-dye bear
- ○ ○ Peanut™, blue elephant †
- ○ ○ Peking™, black/white panda
- ○ ○ Pinchers™, red lobster
- ○ ○ Pinky™, pink flamingo
- ○ ○ Pouch™, brown kangaroo
- ○ ○ Pounce™, brown/cream cat
- ○ ○ Prance™, grey/brown cat
- ○ ○ Princess™, white bear
- ○ ○ Puffer™, black/white puffin
- ○ ○ Pugsly™, black/cream pug
- ○ ○ Quackers™, yellow duck †
- ○ ○ Radar™, black bat
- ○ ○ Rainbow™, tie dye chameleon
- ○ ○ Rex™, tie-dye tyrannosaurus
- ○ ○ Righty™, gray elephant with U.S. flag
- ○ ○ Ringo™, brown raccoon
- ○ ○ Roary™, brown lion
- ○ ○ Rover™, red dog
- ○ ○ Scoop™, blue pelican

BEANIE BABIES® POEMS

Libearty™
I am called libearty
I wear the flag for all to see
Hope and freedom is my way
That's why I wear flag USA

Lizzy™
Lizzy loves Legs the frog
    She hides with him under logs
    Both of them search for flies
Underneath the clear blue skies!

Lucky™
Lucky the lady bug loves the lotto
"Someone must win" that's her motto
But save your dimes and even a penny
Don't spend on the lotto and
You'll have many!

Magic™
Magic the dragon lives in a dream
The most beautiful that you have ever seen
Through magic lands she likes to fly
Look up and watch her, way up high!

Manny™
Manny is sometimes called a sea cow
She likes to twirl and likes to bow
    Manny sure is glad you bought her
    Because it's so lonely under water!

Maple™
Maple the bear likes to ski
With his friends, he plays hockey.
He loves his pancakes and eats every crumb
Can you guess which country he's from?

Mel™
How do you name a Koala bear?
It's rather tough, I do declare!
It confuses me, I get into a funk
I'll name him Mel, after my favorite hunk!

Mystic™
Once upon a time so far away
A unicorn was born one day in May
Keep Mystic with you, she's a prize
You'll see the magic in her blue eyes!

Nana™
No Poem
_____
_____
_____
_____

Nanook™
Nanook is a dog that loves cold weather
To him a sled is light as a feather
Over the snow and through the slush
He runs at hearing the cry of "mush"!

Nip™
His name is Nipper, but we call him Nip
His best friend is a black cat named Zip
Nip likes to run in races for fun
He runs so fast he's always number one!

Nuts™
With his bushy tail, he'll scamper up a tree
The most cheerful critter you'll ever see,
He's nuts about nuts, and he loves to chat
Have you ever seen a squirrel like that?

Patti™
Ran into Patti one day while walking
Believe me she wouldn't stop talking
Listened and listened to her speak
That would explain her extra large beak!

Peace™
All races, all colors, under the sun
Join hands together and have some fun
Dance to the music, rock and roll is the sound
Symbols of peace and love abound!

Peanut™
Peanut the elephant walks on tip toes
Quietly sneaking wherever she goes
She'll sneak up on you and a hug
You will get
Peanut is a friend you won't soon forget!

Peking™
No Poem
_____
_____
_____
_____

BEANIE BABIES® POEMS

Pinchers™

This lobster loves to pinch
Eating his food inch by inch
Balancing carefully with his tail
Moving forward slow as a snail!

Pinky™

Pinky loves the everglades
From the hottest pink she's made
With floppy legs and big orange beak
She's the Beanie that you seek!

Pouch™

My little pouch is handy I've found
It helps me carry my baby around
I hop up and down without any fear
Knowing my baby is safe and near.

Pounce™

Sneaking and slinking down the hall
To pounce upon a fluffy yarn ball
Under the tables, around the chairs
Through the rooms and down the stairs!

Prance™

She darts around and swats the air
Then looks confused when nothing's there
Pick her up and pet her soft fur
Listen closely, and you'll hear her purr!

Princess™

Like an angel, she came from heaven above
She shared her compassion, her pain, her love
She only stayed with us long enough to teach
The world to share, to give, to reach.

Puffer™

What in the world does a puffin do?
We're sure that you would like to know too
We asked Puffer how she spends her days
Before she answered, she flew away!

Pugsly™

Pugsly is picky about what he will wear
Never a spot, a stain or a tear
Image is something of which he'll gloat
Until he noticed his wrinkled coat!

Quackers™

There is a duck by the name of Quackers
Every night he eats animal crackers
He swims in a lake that's clear and blue
But he'll come to the shore to be with you!

Radar™

Radar the bat flies late at night
He can soar to an amazing height
If you see something as high as a star
Take a good look, it might be Radar!

Rainbow™

Red, green, blue and yellow
This chameleon is a colorful fellow.
A blend of colors, his own unique hue
Rainbow was made especially for you!

Rex™

No Poem
_____
_____
_____
_____

Righty™

Donkeys to the left, elephants to the right
Often seems like a crazy sight
This whole game seems very funny
Until you realize they're spending
Your money!

Ringo™

Ringo hides behind his mask
He will come out, if you should ask
He loves to chitter. He loves to chatter
Just about anything, it doesn't matter!

Roary™

Deep in the jungle they crowned him king
But being brave is not his thing
A cowardly lion some may say
He hears his roar and runs away!

Rover™

This dog is red and his name is Rover
If you call him he is sure to come over
He barks and plays with all his might
But worry not, he won't bite!

BEANIE BABIES® POEMS

Scoop™

All day long he scoops up fish
To fill his bill, is his wish
Diving fast and diving low
Hoping those fish are very slow!

Scottie™

Scottie is a friendly sort
Even though his legs are short
He is always happy as can be
His best friends are you and me!

Seamore™

Seamore is a little white seal
Fish and clams are her favorite meal
Playing and laughing in the sand
She's the happiest seal in the land!

Seaweed™

Seaweed is what she likes to eat
It's supposed to be a delicious treat
Have you tried a treat from the water
If you haven't, maybe you "otter"!

Slither™

No Poem

_____
_____
_____

Sly™

Sly is a fox and tricky is he
Please don't chase him, let him be
If you want him, just say when
He'll peek out from his den!

Smoochy™

Is he a frog or maybe a prince?
This confusion makes him wince
Find the answer, help him with this
Be the one to give him a kiss!

Snip™

Snip the cat is Siamese
She'll be your friend if you please
So toss her a toy or a piece of string
Playing with you is her favorite thing!

Snort™

Although Snort is not so tall
He loves to play basketball
He is a star player in his dreams
Can you guess his favorite team?

Snowball™

There is a snowman, I've been told
That plays with Beanies out in the cold
What is better in a winter wonderland
Than a Beanie snowman in your hand!

Sparky™

Sparky rides proud on the fire truck
Ringing the bell and pushing his luck
He gets under foot when trying to help
He often gets stepped on and
Lets out a yelp!

Speedy™

Speedy ran marathons in the past
Such a shame, always last
Now Speedy is a big star
After he bought a racing car!

Spike™

Spike the rhino likes to stampede
He's the bruiser that you need
Gentle to birds on his back and spike
You can be his friend if you like!

Spinner™

Does this spider make you scared?
Among many people that feeling is shared
Remember spiders have feelings too
In fact, this spider really likes you!

Splash™

Splash loves to jump and dive
He's the fastest whale alive
He always wins the 100 yard dash
With a victory jump he'll make a splash!

Spooky™

Ghosts can be a scary sight
But don't let Spooky bring you any fright
Because when you're alone, you will see
The best friend that Spooky can be!

Beanie Babies® Poems

Spot™

See Spot sprint, see Spot run
You and Spot will have lots of fun
Watch out now, because he's not slow
Just stand back and watch him go!

Spunky™
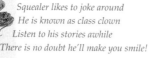
Bouncing around without much grace
To jump on your lap and lick your face
But watch him closely he has no fears
He'll run so fast he'll trip over his ears

Squealer™

Squealer likes to joke around
He is known as class clown
Listen to his stories awhile
There is no doubt he'll make you smile!

Steg™
No Poem
_____
_____
_____

Sting™

I'm a manta ray and my name is Sting
I'm quite unusual and this is the thing
Under the water I glide like a bird
Have you ever seen something so absurd?

Stinky™

Deep in the woods he lived in a cave
Perfume and mints were the gifts he gave
He showered every night in the kitchen sink
Hoping one day he wouldn't stink!

Stretch™

She thinks when her head is underground
The rest of her body can't be found
The Beanie Babies think it's absurd
To play hide and seek with this bird!

Stripes™
Stripes was never fierce nor strong
So with tigers, he didn't get along
Jungle life was hard to get by
So he came to his friends at Ty!

Strut™

Listen closely to "cock-a-doodle-doo"
What's the rooster saying to you?
Hurry, wake up sleepy head
We have lots to do, get out of bed!

Tabasco™

Although Tabasco is not so tall
He loves to play basketball
He is a star player in his dream
Can you guess his favorite team?

Tank™

This armadillo lives in the South
Shoving Tex-Mex in his mouth
He sure loves it south of the border
Keeping his friends in good order!

Teddy™ (brown)

Teddy wanted to go out today
All of his friends went out to play
But he'd rather help whatever you do
After all, his best friend is you!

Teddy™ (cranberry)
No Poem
_____
_____
_____

Teddy™ (jade)
No Poem
_____
_____
_____
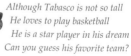

Teddy™ (magenta)
No Poem
_____
_____
_____

Teddy™ (teal)
No Poem
_____
_____
_____

BEANIE BABIES® POEMS

Teddy™ (violet)
No Poem

_____
_____
_____
_____

Waves™

Join him today on the Internet
Don't be afraid to get your feet wet
He taught all the Beanies how to surf
Our web page is his home turf!

Trap™

No Poem

_____
_____
_____

Web™

No Poem

_____
_____
_____

Tuffy™

Taking off with a thunderous blast
Tuffy rides his motorcycle fast
The Beanies roll with laughs and squeals
He never took off his training wheels!

Weenie™

Weenie the dog is quite a sight
Long of body and short of height
He perches himself high on a log
And considers himself to be top dog!

Tusk™

Tusk brushes his teeth everyday
To keep them shiny, it's the only way
Teeth are special, so you must try
And they will sparkle when
You say "Hi"!

Wrinkles™

This little dog is named Wrinkles
His nose is soft and often crinkles
Likes to climb up on your lap
He's a cheery sort of chap!

Twigs™

Twigs has his head in the clouds
He stands tall, he stands proud
With legs so skinny they wobble and shake
What an unusual friend he will make!

Ziggy™

Ziggy likes soccer – he's a referee
That way he watches the games for free
The other Beanies don't think it's fair
But Ziggy the Zebra doesn't care!

Valentino™

His heart is red and full of love
He cares for you so give him a hug
Keep him close when feeling blue
Feel the love he has for you!

Zip™

Keep Zip by your side all the day through
Zip is good luck, you'll see it's true
When you have something you need to do
Zip will always believe in you!

Velvet™

Velvet loves to sleep in the trees
Lulled to dreams by the buzz of the bees
She snoozes all day and plays all night
Running and jumping in the moonlight!

Waddle™

Waddle the Penguin likes to dress up
Every night he wears his tux
When Waddle walks, it never fails
He always trips over his tails!

𝒟o you or any of your friends share a birthday with any of your favorite Beanie Babies?

JANUARY

Jan. 3, 1993 . . . . . . .Spot
Jan. 6, 1993 . . . . . . .Patti
Jan. 13, 1996 . . . . .Crunch
Jan. 14, 1997 . . . . .Spunky
Jan. 15, 1996 . . . . . . .Mel
Jan. 18, 1994 . . . . . .Bones
Jan. 21, 1996 . . . . . . .Nuts
Jan. 25, 1995 . . . . .Peanut
Jan. 26, 1996 . . . . . .Chip

FEBRUARY

Feb. 1, 1996 . . . . . . .Peace
Feb. 13, 1995 . . . . . .Stinky
Feb. 13, 1995 . . . . . .Pinky
Feb. 14, 1994 . . .Valentino
Feb. 17, 1996 . . . . . .Baldy
Feb. 20, 1996 . . . . . .Roary
Feb. 22, 1995 . . . . . . .Tank
Feb. 25, 1994 . . . .Happy
Feb. 27, 1996 . . . .Sparky
Feb. 28, 1995 . . . . . . .Flip

MARCH

March 2, 1995 . . . . . .Coral
March 6, 1994 . . . . . . .Nip
March 8, 1996 . . .Doodle
March 14, 1994 . . . . . .Ally
March 19, 1996 . . .Seaweed
March 21, 1996 . . . .Fleece
March 28, 1994 . . . . . .Zip

APRIL

April 3, 1996 . . . . .Hoppity
April 4, 1997 . . . . . . .Hissy
April 12, 1996 . . . . . . .Curly
April 18, 1995 . . . . . . .Ears
April 19, 1994 . . . .Quackers
April 23, 1993 . . .Squealer
April 25, 1993 . . . . . . .Legs
April 27, 1993 . . .Chocolate

MAY

May 1, 1995 . . . . . . .Lucky
May 1, 1996 . . . . .Wrinkles
May 2, 1996 . . . . . .Pugsly
May 3, 1996 . . . . .Chops
May 10, 1994 . . . . .Daisy
May 11, 1995 . . . . . .Lizzy
May 13, 1993 . . . . . .Flash
May 15, 1995 . . .Tabasco
May 15, 1995 . . . . . .Snort
May 19, 1995 . . . . . .Twigs
May 21, 1994 . . . . . .Mystic
May 28, 1996 . . . .Floppity
May 30, 1996 . . . . . .Rover

JUNE

June 1, 1996 . . . . . .Hippity
June 3, 1996 . . . . .Freckles
June 8, 1995 . . . . . .Bucky
June 8, 1995 . . . . . .Manny
June 11, 1995 . . . . .Stripes
June 15, 1996 . . . . .Scottie
June 17, 1996 . . . . .Gracie
June 19, 1993 . . . .Pinchers
June 27, 1995 . . . . .Bessie

JULY

July 1, 1996 . . . . .Pride
July 1, 1996 . . . . . . .Scoop
July 1, 1996 . . . . . . .Maple
July 2, 1995 . . . . . .Bubbles
July 4, 1996 . . . . .Lefty
July 4, 1996 . . . . . . .Righty
July 8, 1993 . . . . . .Splash
July 14, 1995 . . . . . . .Ringo
July 15, 1994 . . . . .Blackie
July 19, 1995 . . . . . . .Grunt
July 20, 1995 . . . .Weenie

AUGUST

Aug. 1, 1995 . . . . . .Garcia
Aug. 9, 1995 . . . . . . .Hoot
Aug. 12, 1997 . . . . . .Iggy
Aug. 13, 1996 . . . . . .Spike
Aug. 14, 1994 . . . .Speedy
Aug. 17, 1995 . . . . . .Bongo
Aug. 17, 1995 . . . . . .Nana
Aug. 23, 1995 . . . . .Digger
Aug. 27, 1995 . . . . . .Sting
Aug. 28, 1997 . . . .Pounce

SEPTEMBER

Sept. 3, 1995 . . . . . . .Inch
Sept. 3, 1996 . . . .Claude
Sept. 5, 1995 . . . . . .Magic
Sept. 9, 1997 . . . . . .Bruno
Sept. 12, 1996 . . . . . . .Sly
Sept. 16, 1995 . . . . . .Kiwi
Sept. 16, 1995 . . . .Derby
Sept. 18, 1995 . . . . . .Tusk
Sept. 21, 1997 . . . .Stretch

OCTOBER

Oct. 1, 1997 . . . . .Smoochy
Oct. 3, 1996 . . . . . .Bernie
Oct. 9, 1996 . . . . . .Doby
Oct. 12, 1996 . . . . . . .Tuffy
Oct. 14, 1997 . . . .Rainbow
Oct. 16, 1995 . . . . .Bumble
Oct. 17, 1996 . . . . . .Dotty
Oct. 22, 1996 . . . . . .Snip
Oct. 30, 1995 . . . . . .Radar
Oct. 31, 1995 . . . . .Spooky

NOVEMBER

Nov. 3, 1997 . . . . . .Puffer
Nov. 6, 1996 . . . . . .Pouch
Nov. 9, 1996 . . . . . .Congo
Nov. 14, 1993 . . . . .Cubbie
Nov. 14, 1993 . . . .Brownie
Nov. 14, 1994 . . . . .Goldie
Nov. 20, 1997 . . . .Prance
Nov. 21, 1996 . . . .Nanook
Nov. 28, 1995 . . . . .Teddy
Nov. 29, 1994 . . . . . .Inky

DECEMBER

Dec. 2, 1996 . . . . .Jolly
Dec. 8, 1996 . . . . . .Waves
Dec. 12, 1996 . . . .Blizzard
Dec. 14, 1996 . . .Seamore
Dec. 16, 1995 . . . . . .Velvet
Dec. 19, 1995 . . . . .Waddle
Dec. 21, 1996 . . . . . . .Echo
Dec. 24, 1995 . . . . . .Ziggy

Word Search

Find your favorite Beanie Babies® in this challenging word search. There are 20 in all. Happy hunting! (See page 93 for answers)

CURLY
DOBY
ECHO
IGGY
INCH

LEFTY
LUCKY
MEL
NIP
NUTS

PATTI
POUNCE
QUACKERS
RAINBOW
REX

SLY
SMOOCHY
SPOT
SQUEALER
STEG

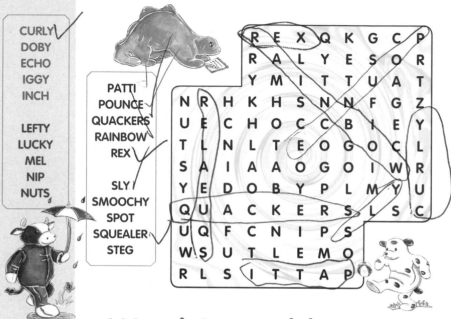

```
R E X Q K G C P
R A L Y E S O R
Y M I T T U A T
N R H K H S N N F G Z
U E C H O C C B I E Y
T L N L T E O G O C L
S A I A A O G O I W R
Y E D O B Y P L M Y U
Q U A C K E R S L S C
U Q F C N I P S
W S U T L E M O
R L S I T T A P
```

Word Scramble

Try to rearrange the letters to spell your favorite Beanie Babies® names. Good luck! (See page 93 for answers)

1. RESNIPHC _____
2. NUPSKY _____
3. LOWALNSB _____
4. NRBOU _____
5. DAULCE _____
6. LOBESBG _____
7. CPSOSO _____
8. ESTOTC _____
9. RECHTST _____
10. NEIEWE _____

11. PRITSES _____
12. NUTAEP _____
13. SIHYS _____
14. ESAEDWE _____
15. NESSCPIR _____
16. RENIPSN _____
17. NOBOG _____
18. RNITANAIB _____
19. EANIVNLTO _____
20. YTPILOFP _____

Maze

Please help Chops the lamb find Bones the dog, but don't forget to stop for treats along the way! (See page 93 for answers)

Start

Finish

My Beanie Babies® Record

U se this page to record the important highlights about your Beanie Babies® collection.

My First Beanie: _____

Where I Got It: _____

When I Got It: _____

My Favorite Beanie: _____

Where I Got It: _____

When I Got It: _____

My Hardest-To-Find Beanie: _____

Where I Got It: _____

When I Got It: _____

My Most Unusual Beanie: _____

Where I Got It: _____

When I Got It: _____

My Most Valuable Beanie: _____

Where I Got It: _____

When I Got It: _____

My Most Wanted Beanies: _____

_____

_____

_____

INDEX BY ANIMAL TYPE

TB = Teenie Beanies
PP = Pillow Pals

COLLECTOR'S
VALUE GUIDE™

Below is an alphabetical listing of the Beanies and the pages you can find them on in the value guide!

GAMES ANSWERS

Answers to Word Search

Answers to Word Scramble

1. Pinchers	8. Scottie
2. Spunky	9. Stretch
3. Snowball	10. Weenie
4. Bruno	11. Stripes
5. Claude	12. Peanut
6. Gobbles	13. Hissy
7. Scoop	14. Seaweed

15. Princess
16. Spinner
17. Bongo
18. Britannia
19. Valentino
20. Floppity

Answer to Maze

Look for these other

Collectors' Publishing
Presents The

CREATE YOUR OWN
DREAM BEANIE
CONTEST

FOR KIDS!!!
FOR ADULTS!!!

Here's How You Enter:

Use your imagination to dream up your very own "Dream Beanie." Pick a name. Create a birthdate. Write a poem. Draw a picture. Monthly winners will be posted on the Collectors' Publishing website (www.collectorspub.com) and a lucky few will get published in the Summer Edition or future editions of the Collector's Value Guide™ for Beanie Babies. Enter as many times as you like by copying this form or using your own blank sheet of paper. Maybe your Beanie will enter Collectors' Publishing's Dream Beanie Hall Of Fame!

HAVE FUN!!!

SHARE YOUR DREAM BEANIE IDEAS WITH COLLECTOR FRIENDS!

Your Name _____

Address _____

_____

Phone _____

Store Where You Buy Your Beanies:

Store Name _____

Town & State _____

Schoolkids:

Age & Grade _____

School Name _____

Town & State _____

MAYBE YOUR DREAM BEANIE WILL BE A WINNER!

Contest Rules:

NO PURCHASE NECESSARY. All submissions become the property of Collectors' Publishing. Winners will be selected by the Collectors' Publishing staff. Due to the volume of entries, submissions are not returnable. All entries must be postmarked no later than December 31, 1998. For a list of winners, write to Collectors' Publishing at P.O. Box 2333, Meriden, CT 06450 or check our website at www.collectorspub.com. Void where prohibited by law.

**COLLECTORS'
PUBLISHING**

My Dream Beanie Is A: Groundhog _(animal, character, etc)_

My Dream Beanie's Name Is: Sleepy

My Dream Beanie's Birthday Is: Feboruary 2, 1998

My Dream Beanie's Poem Is: Don't be bitter
If he sees his shadow + six more
weeks of winter, cause if your sad
He'll come + make you glad

My Dream Beanie Looks Like This: